American Justice 2017

American Justice 2017
The Supreme Court in Crisis

Kimberly Robinson

PENN

UNIVERSITY OF PENNSYLVANIA PRESS

PHILADELPHIA

Copyright © 2017 University of Pennsylvania Press

All rights reserved. Except for brief quotations used for purposes of review
or scholarly citation, none of this book may be reproduced in any form by
any means without written permission from the publisher.

Published by
University of Pennsylvania Press
Philadelphia, Pennsylvania 19104-4112
www.upenn.edu/pennpress

Garrett Epps, Consulting Editor

Printed in the United States of America

A Cataloging-in-Publication record is
available from the Library of Congress

Cover design by John Hubbard

ISBN 978-0-8122-4997-2 hardcover
ISBN 978-0-8122-9475-0 ebook

Contents

Preface

It is odd to say that the absence of something is what defines a thing. That, though, is unquestionably the case for the US Supreme Court's 2016 term—a term defined by a vacancy.

The storied institution is so steeped in tradition that the Court's own website declares that "it is in many respects the same institution that first met in 1790." By statutory edict, the justices kick off each term on the "first Monday in October." For practically all of its more than 225-year history, the justices have near-unanimously worn simple black robes instead of the more ornate attire donned by English judges. Since the late nineteenth century, the justices have engaged in the "Judicial Handshake" before each oral argument to remind themselves that "differences of opinion on the Court [do] not preclude overall harmony of purpose," the website tells us.

In 2016, however, when the justices gathered to hear the term's first arguments, there were only eight instead of the nine we have come to expect. That seat would remain empty for more than half the term. Indeed, the spot at the end of the bench reserved for the Court's newest member had already sat empty for months.

Justice Antonin Scalia died unexpectedly on February 13, 2016, while on a hunting trip at a luxurious Texas ranch. Occurring in a rural community, the news was slow to trickle into Washington. But when it did, it sent shockwaves through the capital. Not only had the seventy-nine-year-old justice been on the Court for nearly thirty years, Justice Scalia was also one of the Court's most well-known justices. A *C-SPAN/PBS* survey recently revealed that only 43 percent of Americans can name even one Supreme Court justice. But Justice Scalia's gripping writing style and vivid language often caught the eye—or ire—of the American public. In one instance, he referred to the Supreme Court's decision to uphold a portion of the Affordable Care Act (also known as Obamacare) as "pure applesauce" and "jiggery-pokery." Another time, he denounced the Court's decision to affirm the right to same-sex marriage by claiming that the Court's reasoning resembled "the mystical aphorisms of the fortune cookie." The decision was so bad, Justice Scalia asserted, that he would have hid his "head in a bag" had he signed onto it. One particularly notable example of dramatic language appeared in Scalia's opinion in a 1990s dispute over after-school use of public facilities by religious organizations. Speaking about the Court's murky "Lemon test," which gauges when the government has become too intertwined with religion in violation of the First Amendment's Establishment Clause, Justice Scalia said this:

> Like some ghoul in a late night horror movie that repeatedly sits up in its grave and shuffles abroad, after

being repeatedly killed and buried, *Lemon* stalks our
Establishment Clause jurisprudence once again, fright-
ening the little children and school attorneys of Center
Moriches Union Free School District. Its most recent
burial, only last Term, was, to be sure, not fully six feet
under: our decision in [*Lee v. Weisman*], conspicuously
avoided using the supposed 'test' but also declined the
invitation to repudiate it. Over the years, however, no
fewer than five of the currently sitting Justices have, in
their own opinions, personally driven pencils through
the creature's heart.

Given Justice Scalia's prominence in American jurisprudence, his death would have loomed large on its own.
But it took center stage in the unforgettable 2016 presidential election after Senate Republicans vowed to block any
nominee put forth by then president Barack Obama. With
almost a year left in Obama's second four-year term, the
Supreme Court became the focus of an unseemly political
battle that cast the Court as just another political body.

It is easy to view the justices that way—nine (or sometimes fewer) junior varsity politicians making some of
society's most consequential decisions based predomi-
nately on their personal and political beliefs. We seem
to receive confirmation of this view every June when the
Court is winding down its annual nine-month term. It is
during this time that the justices frequently hand down a
string of 5–4 decisions on issues that are hotly contested
among the general public. These closely split decisions are
more often than not decided along ideological lines.

The justices, though, do not see themselves this way.
There are no Republican judges or Democratic judges,

Scalia's eventual replacement, Justice Neil Gorsuch, said over and over again during his confirmation hearing. Most, if not all, of the current justices seem to agree. Part of their job—in addition to deciding some of the nation's most consequential issues—is to defend the integrity of the institution as not just another political branch. It is not a new concept. Alexander Hamilton famously wrote in *Federalist* no. 78 that the judiciary has "neither force nor will, but merely judgment." The judiciary must "ultimately depend upon the aid of the executive arm even for the efficacy of its judgments," Hamilton declared. He warned that as the "weakest of the three departments of power," the judiciary must take "all possible care . . . to enable it to defend itself against" the attacks of the executive and legislative branches.

Despite this long-held conviction—perhaps most prominently expressed today by Chief Justice John Roberts Jr.—the recent Court has not always taken "all possible care" to defend its reputation with the American people. Rightly or wrongly, the Court's decisions regarding the 2000 presidential election, campaign finance, health care, and same-sex marriage have undermined the citizenry's confidence in the institution.

These and other controversial decisions led to a crisis during the Court's 2016 term. In October term 2016, as it is known by court watchers, the Court was seemingly hijacked by the political branches. Caught in a power struggle between the Republican-held Senate and the outgoing Democratic president regarding who would fill the seat left vacant by the death of Justice Scalia, the current justices were forced to press on through nearly an entire term shorthanded.

While the political spotlight was focused on the Supreme Court, scuttling any attempt to describe the court in apolitical terms, what did the justices do? Instead of publicly lobbying the American people or calling attention to the difficulties caused by the vacancy, they went on with their work, acting as if business was proceeding as usual while the confirmation battle played out. In public, the justices responded that they would just "deal with it" when asked about the shorthanded Court. In private, they likely struggled to present the Court as a functioning branch of government. True, no one can know for sure. The inner workings of the prestigious institution are obscured by secrecy. But narrow outcomes, historically low output, and the ducking of consequential issues hint at the strenuous effort the eight justices made to uphold the integrity of the institution.

This fourth book in the *American Justice* series tells the story of how the Court ended up in this crisis, how it dealt with the tumultuous situation, and where it is likely to go from here.

The book starts with the compelling tale of Gavin Grimm, a transgender Virginia teenager. The case turns out to the perfect example of the effects of the vacancy on the Supreme Court term—with odd procedural maneuvering and the avoidance of contentious issues that threatened to split the shorthanded Court 4–4. But the case did not start out that way, making it a captivating introduction into the Court's 2016 term.

The story continues with the retelling of the dramatic political hijacking of the Supreme Court—from GOP leaders vowing to hold off President Obama's Supreme Court nominee just hours after word of Justice Scalia's death had surfaced to the bitter confirmation of his eventual successor, Justice Gorsuch.

Then this narrative takes a deep dive into how the justices dealt with the resulting crisis. One way was to deftly avoid divisive issues that could split the Court evenly and confirm its status as just another political branch. Deciding cases on extremely limited grounds—likely the only way the Court could garner a majority of justices—was another. Chapters 3 and 4 examine how the Court deployed these methods in cases dealing with issues as consequential as the separation of church and state and the right to vote to those as run-of-the-mill as insider trading and credit card fees.

The lens then gets broader as I explain how the Court got into the crisis in the first place. Procedurally abnormal and widely unpopular judicial decisions led the Court into its most notorious crisis: FDR's court-packing plan. But despite that cautionary tale, the Roberts Court has veered onto a similar path. Chapter 5 looks at how the Court has used the First Amendment as a weapon to invalidate widely supported laws—an approach that contributed to the crisis in which the Court was embroiled for much of its 2016 term.

Chapters 6 and 7 demonstrate that even the most carefully orchestrated plans sometimes go off the rails. The Court was essentially forced into the blockbuster fight over President Donald Trump's travel ban. The result was a much-anticipated but infinitely puzzling order that seemed to give both sides the opportunity to claim victory. But the justices also jumped into a less prominent, if no less consequential, dispute over hot-button criminal justice issues. The Court's ostensibly voluntary foray into capital punishment, race in the criminal justice system, and law enforcement abuses stand in contrast to the rest of the term's efforts to skirt controversial issues.

Finally, with a fully staffed bench, the Court now seems primed to leap back into the political fray. Taking cases dealing with such weighty issues as how legislatures draw voting districts, whether religious believers can exempt themselves from antidiscrimination laws, and the constitutionality of President Trump's controversial travel ban, the Court's 2017 term is shaping up to be a blockbuster. Should the Court continue with such aggressive dockets in future terms, that could lead it into paralysis yet again. Whether that happens will depend, of course, on how strongly the newly reconstituted conservative majority flexes its muscles—and whether the Court's longstanding ideological make-up is upset by any retirements, unexpected illnesses, or deaths. Such events are now all that stands between a fully functional Court and the kind of crisis that impeded it in 2016.

Trench Warfare

Anyone who is a parent—or really, anyone who has ever been a teenager—is likely to find Gavin Grimm's Supreme Court case to be sympathetic. Sympathetic because the case involves a teenager. More sympathetic because it involves a transgender teen. And even more sympathetic because it has implications for the future of a group of kids more likely to commit suicide than their peers. But courts have the difficult task of weighing the needs of the few against the needs of the many. Known in the legal world as "balancing the equities," the idea suggests that the extreme hardship of the few can be outweighed by the less-threatening, yet more broadly felt harms to the vast majority. And when that vast majority itself consists of uncertain teens, sympathies get muddied. Which brings us to Grimm's case, formally known in the US Supreme Court as *Gloucester County School Board v. G. G.*

Gloucester County was a microcosm of the high court's 2016 term—a term fundamentally shaped by the unseemly political battle that unfolded after the shocking death of longtime Justice Antonin Scalia. The clash left the Supreme Court shorthanded for more than a year and impacted not only the kinds of cases the justices took but also the way that they resolved them. In particular, the justices batted away contentious issues that threatened to split the evenly numbered Court 4–4 and cast it even more as a political institution. Ultimately, that was what happened in *Gloucester County*.

But it did not start out that way.

In August 2016, two months before the high court would kick off its 2016 term, Grimm was getting ready to start his senior year of high school. The insecurities and uncertainties surrounding such a momentous time were likely amplified by the fact that Grimm is a transgender boy—that is, Grimm was born a girl but identifies as a boy.

Grimm had been diagnosed with gender dysphoria, a "conflict between a person's physical or assigned gender and the gender with which he/she/they identify," according to the American Psychiatric Association (APA), which publishes the authoritative Diagnostic and Statistical Manual of Mental Health Disorders. "People with gender dysphoria may often experience significant distress and/or problems functioning associated with this conflict between the way they feel and think of themselves (referred to as experienced or expressed gender) and their physical or assigned gender," the APA said.

In his filings with the Supreme Court, Grimm said that he has consulted with a doctor about his gender dysphoria. As a result, he received testosterone hormone therapy and underwent chest reconstruction surgery. Moreover, he legally changed his name and obtained an amended birth certificate that indicated that he was a male. Grimm "appears no different from any other boy his age and uses the men's restrooms at restaurants, shopping malls, the doctor's office, the library, movie theaters, and government buildings," his Supreme Court filings said.

"Socially transitioning primarily involves transitioning into the affirmed gender's pronouns and bathrooms," the APA says. That was probably why Grimm and his mother approached school officials before his sophomore year. Those officials, according to one federal court, "were supportive and took steps to ensure that he would be treated as a boy by teachers and staff." That included allowing Grimm to use the boys' restroom, just as he did when he was in public.

That, however, was short-lived. Seven weeks into the arrangement, members of the community reached out to the Gloucester County School Board, seeking to bar Grimm from the boys' bathroom. The school board addressed the complaints during two school board meetings in late 2014. Dozens of people spoke at these meetings, many of whom "displayed hostility" toward Grimm, a federal court reviewing Grimm's case said. Speakers referred to Grimm "as a 'girl' or young lady," the court said. One speaker called Grimm "a 'freak' and compared him to a person who thinks he is a 'dog' and wants to urinate on fire hydrants."

Eventually, on December 9, 2014, the school board voted 6–1 to override the school's policy. Students must use bathrooms that correspond to their gender at birth, the school board declared. Students like Grimm, who were unable to use such bathrooms given their gender dysphoria, would be allowed to use a separate, unisex, single-stall bathroom.

Grimm's case would ultimately wind up at the Supreme Court. But that was certainly not where his attorney, Josh Block of the American Civil Liberties Union (ACLU), initially saw it going. At every step, he thought the school board would back down. Usually once the school board's attorneys get involved, they would decide this was not the kind of fight they wanted to have, Block said.

So Block filed a demand letter with the school board, seeking to quash the policy. It failed. He filed a complaint with the Department of Justice. That did too. Eventually, he sued the school district in federal court.

Grimm argued that the school board's resolution violated Title IX of the Education Amendments Act of 1972. That law prohibits schools from discriminating against students based on their "sex." Under the Obama administration, the Department of Education said that sex discrimination includes discrimination against transgender students.

The school board, however, said in court documents that it did not adopt the policy "in an attempt to stigmatize, embarrass, or otherwise reject [Grimm]. . . . Instead, in an effort to accommodate [Grimm, as well as] take into account the legitimate safety and privacy interests of [Grimm] and all the other Gloucester County Schools' students," the school board built three unisex, single-stall bathrooms. "Any student can use these single-stall bathrooms, regardless of their biological sex, if they are uncomfortable using a communal bathroom, or for any other private, personal reason," the school board said in court documents.

After more than a year of litigation and some initial setbacks, the federal courts agreed with Grimm, and he won a court order allowing him to use his school's boys' restroom once again. It was just in time for his senior year. But then the Supreme Court stepped in. In a one-paragraph order issued August 3, the high court halted that decision. Grimm would now start his senior year without the benefit he had won in the lower courts.

The decision split the shorthanded Court 5–3. Surprisingly, Justice Stephen Breyer joined the Court's Republican-appointed justices in ruling against Grimm. The fact that he joined the Court's more conservative bloc was not itself a shock. Justice Breyer, a Clinton appointee, occasionally parts from his Democrat-appointed colleagues, especially in criminal matters. It was the reason that Justice Breyer gave for coming down the way he did that was odd: he was voting to stop the lower courts' rulings as a "courtesy" to his conservative colleagues.

A brief sojourn into the morass of Supreme Court procedure is necessary here. The so-called courtesy fifth vote is the product of the Supreme Court's rules regarding how many justices it takes to get certain things done at the high court. The Supreme Court does not have to—and certainly does not—take every case that comes before it. Instead, the Court will only hear a case if four of the nine justices vote to do so, known as voting to grant certiorari, or cert. But it takes a majority of the justices—five—to grant a "stay" like the one at issue in Grimm's case. Such stays merely pause lower court decisions.

In a routine case, the incongruity between the number of votes required to hear a case and to pause a lower court ruling causes no problems. But in capital cases, the rules create a macabre possibility. Say four justices want to hear a death row inmate's case, but they cannot convince another justice to stay the impending execution. The execution itself will moot the case before the Supreme Court gets a chance to hear it. The courtesy fifth vote comes to the rescue. If four justices indicate that they would like to hear a capital case, another justice—typically the chief justice—will agree to vote to stay the execution until the Court can consider the dispute.

While the courtesy fifth vote was intended to address capital cases, Justice Breyer's vote in *Gloucester County* sought to extend its use to civil ones—that is, those cases that do not involve criminal matters. It is unclear why Justice Breyer wanted to do so. Although Chief Justice John Roberts Jr. has called the Supreme Court the most transparent branch of government, most of the Court's work is actually shrouded in mystery. But observers can guess that Justice Breyer, staring down potentially an entire term with only eight justices, wanted to engender a more cooperative atmosphere among the group. As Justice Samuel Alito Jr. would later put it, having eight justices was "awkward" and "unusual." It required the justices to spend more time coming to a consensus and resulted in narrower decisions, Justice Alito said at a conference in April, according to Jess Bravin of the *Wall Street Journal*.

If intended to bring about more collegiality, there were outward signs that Justice Breyer's courtesy vote paid off, at least in the criminal context. During his confirmation hearings in 2005, Roberts, now a chief justice, spoke approvingly of the use of the courtesy fifth vote. "I don't want to commit to pursue a particular practice," the chief justice said, but "I think that practice makes a lot of sense." However, that custom seemed to have fallen out of favor in recent terms. In November 2014, the Supreme Court denied Missouri death row inmate Leo Taylor's request to stay his execution. At the same time, the Court denied his petition for cert. The Court's liberal bloc—Justices Ruth Bader Ginsburg, Breyer, Sonia Sotomayor, and Elena Kagan—noted that they voted to stay the execution but were overruled by the Court's conservatives. Curiously, there was no noted dissent to the denial of cert. Because there were not four votes to grant cert, the courtesy fifth vote was not technically broken. It is unclear, though, why the dissenting justices would have granted a stay if they did not think the underlying issue was worth the Court's time. What is more likely is that they wanted to hear the case but did not note their dissent publicly.

Following Justice Breyer's courtesy vote in *Gloucester County*, the practice appeared to resurface. In November 2016, several months after the stay in Grimm's case, Chief Justice Roberts voted to halt an imminent Alabama execution despite the fact that, in his opinion, the case did not meet the Court's "ordinary criteria for a stay." The claims are "purely fact-specific, dependent on contested interpretations of state law, insulated from our review by alternative holdings below, or some combination of the three," Chief Justice Roberts wrote. "Four justices have, however, voted to grant a stay. To afford them the opportunity to more fully consider the suitability of this case for review, including these circumstances, I vote to grant the stay as a courtesy." Justice Breyer had emerged victorious in his quest to restore collegiality . . . at least temporarily.

The Supreme Court's stay in Grimm's case all but guaranteed that the justices would agree to take up the case.

That was because one of the major factors that the Court looks to when deciding whether to stay lower courts' decisions is whether the case presents a "cert-worthy" issue that the justices are likely to hear. By saying that the stay was warranted in Grimm's case, the justices essentially said that the issue was one they would like to take a look at. And indeed, they did. Less than a month into the 2016 term, the Supreme Court granted the school board's request to review the decision below, and oral argument was set for March 2017.

Grimm's Supreme Court filings attempt to describe the price of that collegiality to him personally. Given the length it takes to hear and resolve a Supreme Court case, the stay nearly assured that Grimm would not be allowed to use the boys' restroom during his final year of high school. As a result, "Grimm does everything he can to avoid using the restroom," according to his Supreme Court filings. "[He] has developed painful urinary tract infections and is distracted and uncomfortable in class. If Grimm has to use the restroom, he uses the nurse's restroom, but he feels ashamed doing so," those filings detail. "It makes him feel 'like a walking freak show' and 'a public spectacle' before the entire community."

What was at issue in Grimm's case depends on whom you ask. For many, it was about privacy for some of our most vulnerable members of society: students. Longtime conservative Judge Paul Niemeyer compellingly described what was at issue for these students when the case was before a lower federal court. "Bodily privacy is historically one of the most basic elements of human dignity and individual freedom," Niemeyer explained. Forcing "a person of one biological sex to be exposed to persons of the opposite biological sex profoundly offends this dignity and freedom." He noted that society has "universally condemned as inhumane such forced exposure throughout history as it occurred in various contexts, such as in prisons." All of that was lost in the "service of the politically correct acceptance of gender identification as the meaning of 'sex,'" Niemeyer lamented.

But, he said, these "longstanding norms are not a protest against persons who identify with a gender different from their biological sex. To the contrary, schools and the courts must, with care, seek to understand their condition and address it in permissible ways that are as helpful as possible in the circumstances. But that is not to say that, to do so, we must bring down all protections of bodily privacy that are inherent in individual human dignity and freedom," Niemeyer concluded.

For others, though, the case was not about student privacy as much as it was an important administrative law issue regarding how much deference courts should give to administrative agencies when interpreting their own rules. That is an important question, to be sure, as administrative agencies—frequently called the fourth branch of government—touch nearly all aspects of American life. The Environmental Protection Agency determines the responsibility that states and businesses have for clean air and water. Several agencies, including the Treasury Department, the Consumer Financial Protection Bureau, and the Securities and Exchange Commission, largely determine the stability—or instability—of our financial system. And the Food and Drug Administration protects the safety of our medical drugs and food supply. Those are just a few of the hundreds of federal administrative agencies that churn out regulations for the rest of us to follow.

For Grimm, though, the case was about getting courts and, more importantly, society to understand who transgender kids are, his attorney, Block, said. Grimm's goal all along was not just to advocate for himself but to prevent his situation from happening to other transgender kids. More broadly, it was about exposing the world to transgender kids and gaining acceptance in society, Block described.

All of those interests are significant and worthy of the high court's time. But the Supreme Court routinely turns away such weighty issues. Between seven thousand and eight thousand cases are brought before the Supreme Court each term. Very few of those mandate the Supreme Court's involvement. In litigation between the states or cases involving specific important issues like redistricting, there are rules essentially requiring the Court to step in. But for every other kind of case, the Supreme Court can turn them away without any legal consequences for future litigation. In turning away a high-profile voter ID case, the chief justice went out of his way to write a separate statement "respecting the denial of certiorari." Roberts said, it "is important to recall our frequent admonition that '[t]he denial of a writ of certiorari imports no expression of opinion upon the merits of the case.'" As a result, the Supreme Court turns away 99 percent of the cases that it is asked to review, hearing somewhere around seventy cases each term.

In picking the select few cases that they will hear, the justices have said that "circuit splits" are the sine qua non of a cert-worthy petition. There are thirteen federal circuit courts. Those are appellate courts that hear issues from the nearly one hundred district courts that do the federal judiciaries' day-to-day work. Cases from the district courts go to the circuit courts. Cases from the circuit courts can go to the Supreme Court. But circuit courts are not bound by the decisions of their sister circuits. As such, a circuit court in one part of the country could interpret federal law to require one thing, while a circuit court in another part of the country could interpret federal law to require something else. And there you have a circuit split. The Supreme Court often uses such splits as an indication that a particular issue requires the Court's attention. After all, if the lower federal courts agree on how the law is supposed to work, there is no need for the Supreme Court to get involved, Justice Ginsburg has said.

Grimm's case, though, did not involve a circuit split. In fact, the circuit that decided Grimm's case—the Fourth Circuit, which hears cases from Maryland, North Carolina, South Carolina, Virginia, and West Virginia—was the first circuit to even consider the issue, according to Grimm's brief. The justices should let the issue "percolate" in the circuit courts before weighing in, Grimm told the Court. That way, they would have the reasoned opinions of several other federal judges before taking the issue up themselves and establishing a rule that would bind the entire country.

That was not, however, what happened. And those diverging interests—privacy, deference to agencies, and transgender rights—played out in more than five dozen briefs filed with the Court. Most of those were friend-of-the court briefs, often referred to as amicus briefs by Supreme Court watchers. Many of those briefs pitted predictable groups against one another. Law professors weighed in on both sides of the issue, as did coalitions of US states and former members of Congress. Frequent Supreme Court amici weighed in on their expected sides, including the libertarian think tank the Cato Institute and the progressive Constitutional Accountability Center. But some unexpected groups weighed in too. Big businesses, like Apple and Microsoft, faced off against major religious organizations, like the US Conference of Catholic Bishops and the Union of Orthodox Jewish Congregations of America. The technology companies filed an amicus brief in support of Grimm to fight against discriminatory policies that they said adversely affected their businesses, employees, and customers and undermined their "ability to build and maintain the diverse and inclusive workplaces that are essential to the success of their companies." The religious groups banded together despite "disagreements on many points of faith" to predict "sharp clashes with religious belief and practice that will arise if the Court interprets the term 'sex' in Title IX to include gender identity." Such clashes would implicate the religious groups' constitutionally protected right to freely practice their religions, they told the justices.

As well as reflecting the tension between the two sides' legal positions, the amicus briefs also highlighted the emotional tensions between those on opposite sides of this issue. Mark Joseph Stern, who covers the Supreme Court for the liberal-leaning website *Slate*, first noticed that two amici filing in support of the school district identified Grimm in the case caption—the name by which the case is known—as a girl. In particular, the Liberty Counsel and the Center for Constitutional Jurisprudence filed amicus briefs on behalf of their clients that identified Grimm in the case caption as "G.G. by her next friend and mother, DEIRDRE GRIMM." This accurately reflects how courts refer to juveniles—by their initials and through their parent or guardian. But the official case caption for Grimm's case identified him as a boy: "G.G. by *his* next friend." The two amici had taken it upon themselves to recaption the case to reflect their views of Grimm's gender.

That prompted a slight rebuke from the Supreme Court clerk's office. Supreme Court rules state that "your cover is to reflect the caption of the case. Please ensure careful compliance with this requirement in this and other cases in the future," the clerk wrote to the lawyers filing the briefs. Stern did not think that reprimand went far enough. "By misgendering Grimm, these briefs clearly reflect the kind of animus that moved the school board to bar Grimm from the correct bathroom in the first place," he wrote in *Slate*. As such, they should be stricken by the Court and refused any consideration by the justices, Stern argued.

Not everyone agreed. Ed Whelan, of the conservative magazine *National Review*, blogged that the Supreme Court rules do not actually say what the clerk said they did. Rule 34 only requires that briefs include a "caption of the case as appropriate in this Court." But by the end of his blog post, Whelan turned away from purely procedural arguments, seeming to also take issue with referring to Grimm as a boy. "I'd rather not get into the details, so let's just say that the usual defining signs of a female's sex remain unchanged," Whelan concluded.

Perhaps it was because of this charged nature of the dispute that the Supreme Court jumped ship as soon as the opportunity presented itself. There are times when the Court really has no choice but to dismiss a case after it has agreed to hear it. But the justices do not like to do so. That is probably because it is seen as a waste of time and energy for not only the parties and the Court but also the numerous amici. Still, sometimes that is what is required. For example, the Court tossed out one disability rights case, *Ivy v. Morath*, during its 2016 term after it was already set for oral argument. The justices did not explain why they did so; they simply issued an order instructing the lower court to dismiss the case as moot. But a brief filed by the respondent sheds light on the likely reason for the Court's decision. The individuals complaining about the actions in that case had all gotten the ultimate relief they wanted—obtaining a driver's license—or had moved out of the jurisdiction whose actions they were challenging. That essentially tied the Court's hands, as there was no longer a constitutionally required "case or controversy" between the parties.

But that was not what happened in *Gloucester County*. Remember that the case started under the Obama administration. After the stunning results of the 2016 presidential election, it was unclear if the Trump administration would keep in place the Department of Education guidance that the lower courts had relied on when initially ruling in Grimm's favor. On February 22, that uncertainty was put to rest. In a letter to the Supreme Court clerk's office, the Office of the Solicitor General—the executive branch's top lawyer at the Supreme Court—notified the Court that the administration was withdrawing the Obama-era guidance to "consider further and more completely the legal issues involved"—namely, whether Title IX's prohibition against "sex" discrimination included discrimination against transgender students.

The next day, the Supreme Court requested that "the parties submit their views on how this case should proceed in light of the guidance document issued by the Department of Education and Department of Justice on February 22, 2017." Despite the request, the writing was on the wall. The Court seemed destined to dismiss the case and send it back to the lower court.

The parties, however, urged the justices to hang on to the case. In deciding to hear it, the justices had agreed to consider two issues. The first was the administrative law question: Did the lower court properly defer to the Department of Education's interpretation of Title IX? That issue was no longer relevant given the new guidance. But the Court had also agreed to consider the underlying statutory question for itself—that is, even without deferring to the Department of Education's interpretation, did Title IX prohibit discrimination against transgender students? The court's consideration of that issue was unchanged by the withdrawal of guidance, the parties argued. They pointed out that the Trump administration did not take a stance on what Title IX required; it merely wanted to "further and more completely" consider the issue. Without any guidance from the executive, "the Court will inevitably have to settle the question by clarifying the proper interpretation of Title IX," Grimm's attorneys argued. Resolution of the issue now "will save the parties—as well as public and private parties involved in similar disputes throughout the Nation—enormous litigation costs as well as needless and divisive political controversy," the school board's attorneys told the Court.

The Supreme Court did not agree. On March 6, it vacated the decision below and remanded the case back to the lower court to basically start over without the benefit of the Department of Education's guidance. Instead of having the issue decided by the highest court of the land, the issue would play out in local school districts across the country. "Trench warfare," as Grimm's attorney called it. For the time that the political battle over the Supreme Court's vacancy left the justices shorthanded, the country would be forced to handle many of its most pressing legal issues in this way—that is, without the definitive say of the US Supreme Court.

The Stolen Seat

In 1803, in the landmark case *Marbury v. Madison*, the Supreme Court declared that it was "emphatically the province and duty of the judicial department to say what the law is." Though the idea was bold more than two centuries ago, it has come to be a truism of the Supreme Court ever since. So why would the Court, by its own terms tasked with resolving disputes over laws' meanings, seemingly want to stay out of such consequential and controversial issues as the ones at the heart of *Gloucester County*? The answer has become clear: the Supreme Court had been hijacked by a polarizing political dispute in the more political branches of government.

This political battle over an unexpected vacancy left the high court shorthanded for most of the 2016 term. Many argued that it was no big deal. Sure, the Court might be evenly split in a few cases, leaving the law unclear. But a full bench would eventually be able to resolve such issues when the vacancy was filled. True. The real danger, though, was not that the Court might split

4–4 in a handful of cases. It was that the political struggle over who would occupy a Supreme Court seat could give the public the impression that the Court itself was a political institution. Such a conclusion threatened to call into question the Court's legitimacy and the legitimacy of its decisions.

It all began on February 13, 2016.

That was when the legal world was rocked by word of the death of longtime Justice Antonin Scalia. In his nearly thirty years on the high court bench, Justice Scalia transformed the way the legal community approached statutory interpretation—that is, the way that judges and lawyers read the laws that govern our everyday conduct. Comments by Justice Kagan in November 2015 illustrated the point. Justice Kagan, an Obama appointee who was frequently on the opposite side of Justice Scalia in cases that split the Court 5–4—said Justice Scalia "ushered in a change of attitudes" about statutory interpretation. "Old-time statutory interpretation," as she called it, relied on so-called legislative history, including such things as statements made by individual senators at the time the law was being debated. During Justice Scalia's tenure on the Court, "the center of gravity . . . moved toward the kinds of things he's preached for quite some time," Justice Kagan said—namely, textualism. Textualism is the idea that judges should start to interpret a statute's meaning by first looking to the text. Only if the text is ambiguous, or leads to absurd results, should judges move on to other clues on the statute's meaning. Judges vary quite a bit about what they find ambiguous or absurd and what other sources they will consult. But most of them now start with the text, and to that extent, "we're all textualists now," Justice Kagan said, adding that Justice Scalia would be remembered as one of the most important justices in the history of the Supreme Court.

She was not exaggerating. Along with deciphering constitutional provisions, statutory interpretation is at the core of what judges do. Of the sixty-nine cases the Supreme Court decided during its 2016 term, approximately 70 percent included issues of statutory interpretation. Those ranged from questions with far-reaching implications like whether Title IX prohibits discrimination against transgender students—the issue in Grimm's case—to relatively inconsequential issues like whether Federal National Mortgage Association, better known as Fannie Mae, can always remove a case from state court to federal court based on its statutory "sue-and-be-sued clause." (It cannot.) Changing the way judges understand the process of making such determinations has left a major mark on the legal community.

So Justice Scalia's absence on the bench was sure to be felt by many. It was conservatives, though, who would feel the loss most acutely. The "Roberts Court," as the court is known under Chief Justice Roberts, has a reputation for being a conservative court. In reality, it is quite unpredictable. When Justice Scalia was on the bench, it was divided between four reliably *conservative* justices, four reliably *liberal* justices, and Justice Anthony M. Kennedy. Close cases often depended on which way Justice Kennedy would vote. It was really the Kennedy Court, UCLA law professor Adam Winkler once told me. With Justice Scalia's death, however, the Court's ideological makeup seemed destined to shift. According to Stanford law professor Pam Karlan, the Court was on the verge of having a majority of the justices appointed by a Democratic president for the first time in more than forty-five years.

Senate Majority Leader Mitch McConnell, a Kentucky Republican, had other ideas. Like the more than eight hundred other lifetime appointments to the federal bench, the Constitution directs that the president "shall nominate" a Supreme Court candidate with the "Advice and Consent" of the Senate. The Senate first required a Supreme Court nominee to appear before its Judiciary Committee in 1925, according the Senate Historical Office. "Harlan Fiske Stone's appearance was brief, but the senatorial questioning was vigorous," the Senate's website says about that inaugural hearing. The court has vacillated in subsequent years between requiring nominees to appear before the committee and not summoning such nominees. But since "the 1955 nomination of John Marshall Harlan, all Supreme Court appointees have appeared before the Judiciary Committee," the website disclosed. Nevertheless, just about an hour after confirmation of Justice Scalia's death reached Washington, McConnell vowed not to hold confirmation hearings for any Supreme Court nominee until after the 2016 presidential election. "The American people should have a voice in the selection of their next Supreme Court justice," McConnell said. Through their votes for the next president, the people would decide whether that spot was filled by a Democrat or a Republican, he declared.

It was a risky move, to be sure. The Republican primaries were just beginning, and the nomination was still up in the air—or at least, many members of the GOP establishment hoped it was. Then candidate Donald Trump had surprisingly come in second in Iowa's first-in-the-country

Republican caucus. And while Trump would go on to win by large margins in many Super Tuesday races just a few weeks later, his nomination as the GOP's presidential candidate was far from certain. Still, he seemed to have a momentum pushing him toward the eventual nomination. For McConnell's plan to end up with a conservative selected for Justice Scalia's seat, he would have had to have believed that Trump would prevail over likely Democratic candidate Hillary Clinton in November. As Republican Senator Lindsey Graham would later put it during eventual nominee Neil Gorsuch's Supreme Court confirmation hearings, "Obviously" many did not see that happening.

McConnell nevertheless pressed on. As support for the blockade, McConnell and other Republicans pointed to the so-called Biden Rule, named for then senator Joe Biden. In June 1992, Biden gave a speech on the Senate floor, urging President George H. W. Bush to hold off on nominating anyone to the Supreme Court bench should an opening arise during the election season. His speech came several months after the dramatic confirmation hearing of Justice Clarence Thomas, who was accused during his confirmation hearing of sexually harassing a colleague. The allegation and accompanying testimony by his accuser prompted Justice Thomas to call the confirmation process a "circus" and "a national disgrace." "And from my standpoint, as a black American . . . it is a high-tech lynching for uppity blacks who in any way deign to think for themselves, to do for themselves, to have different ideas, and it is a message that unless you kowtow to an old order, this is what will happen to you. You will be lynched, destroyed, caricatured by a committee of the U.S. Senate rather than hung from a tree," Justice Thomas emphatically pronounced. "Given the unusual rancor that prevailed in the Thomas nomination" and "the need for some serious reevaluation of the nomination and confirmation process," Biden urged the Senate to consider refusing to consider any Supreme Court nominee should one be put forth. While the suggestion garnered a strong rebuke from South Carolina's Republican Senator Strom Thurmond, no Supreme Court vacancy emerged during that election, and the issue went away.

Until February 2016, that was. Republicans latched on to the "Biden Rule" as incontrovertible evidence that Scalia's seat should be filled by the next president. Democrats averred that Republicans would be violating their constitutional duties if they did not evaluate the president's nominee. They urged the president to press forward despite the partisanship that had engulfed the issue. Republicans countered; Democrats responded. And on and on it went. All eyes then turned to President Barack Obama. Would he nominate a progressive candidate to help fire up the Democratic voters in the upcoming presidential election? Or would he nominate someone more moderate to try to entice Republicans out of their obstructionist stance?

On March 16, 2016, surrounded by burgeoning cherry blossoms in the Rose Garden, Obama nominated longtime federal judge Merrick Garland to succeed Justice Scalia to the US Supreme Court. Garland had previously been suggested by Republicans as a consensus nominee. Indeed, days before Garland's nomination, Senator Orin Hatch predicted that Obama would nominate a "decidedly liberal candidate" to ensure a Democratic presidential victory when he "could easily name Merrick Garland, who is a fine man," according to John Gizzi of the conservative-leaning

Newsmax magazine. Garland was a former federal prosecutor who led the investigation into and prosecution of the Oklahoma City bombers. He was also a nearly twenty-year veteran of the prominent DC Circuit, considered by many to be the second most important federal court in the country. Garland was imminently qualified for the job of Supreme Court justice. His recommendation from the American Bar Association, which gave him their highest rating of "Well Qualified," noted one colleague as saying that Garland "may be the perfect human being."

Unimpeachable credentials did not change McConnell's mind. The ploy to keep such a qualified and respected individual off the bench initially seemed unworkable. With nearly eight months remaining until the presidential election, it was likely that Republicans up for reelection would face an onslaught of criticism over their opposition to such a qualified candidate. But with only a few hiccups along the way, Republicans stayed mostly united in their opposition to holding hearings for the sixty-three-year-old jurist.

One early and steadfast Republican dissent from this plan was Maine Senator Susan Collins. Collins, who had represented the Pine Tree State for two decades, was a moderate Republican. In her time as a senator, she had supported same-sex marriage, opposed the Partial-Birth Abortion Ban Act, and stated that President Trump's ban on travel for individuals from certain Muslim-majority countries was wrong. On Garland, Collins once again went against her Republican colleagues. The Senate "should follow the regular order in considering [Garland]," Collins told NPR's Robert Siegel. "The Constitution's very clear that the president has every right to make this nomination, and then the Senate can either consent or withhold its consent. The only way that we can do that is by thoroughly vetting the nominee, and that means having personal meetings" and holding a public hearing, she said. The only other Republican to agree with Collins was Illinois Senator Mark Kirk, who was running in a tight race with Democrat Tammy Duckworth—a race he eventually lost.

Two additional senators briefly supported holding confirmation hearings for Garland before succumbing to harsh pressure to fall back in line. Shortly after Obama nominated Garland, Kansas Senator Jerry Moran said that the Senate should hold confirmation hearings. "I would rather have you [constituents] complaining to me that I voted wrong on nominating somebody than saying I'm not doing my job," Moran said at town hall meeting, according to the *Garden City Telegram*. Several days later, he changed his mind. He had "examined Judge Garland's record and didn't need hearings to conclude that the nominee's judicial philosophy, disregard for Second Amendment rights, and sympathy for federal government bureaucracy [made] Garland unacceptable to serve on the Supreme Court," Moran said in a statement. Moran's reversal was reportedly due to intense pressure from conservative groups, which threatened to run a right-wing candidate to challenge the first-term senator in the primary. Alaska Senator Lisa Murkowski also reversed her stance on hearings for Garland after initially seeming to support them.

Liberal groups were similarly united in their *support* of confirmation hearings for Judge Garland. Democratic politicians lambasted their colleagues, urging them to "do their job" and hold hearings for the distinguished jurist.

They did everything they could to try to put the debate over the vacancy at the forefront of voters' minds. They held mock confirmation hearings, organized several rallies on the Supreme Court's sprawling plaza, and delivered impassioned floor speeches in Congress chastising the GOP.

By the time the Garland blockade had stretched into its second month, liberal theories abounded regarding ways Obama could skirt the Senate—or at least the Senate Judiciary Committee. One early and obvious suggestion was a recess appointment. "The Framers adopted the Recess Appointments Clause, without debate, to prevent governmental paralysis," the conservative Heritage Foundation said on its website. Because early sessions of Congress lasted only a few months, "with Senators dispersing throughout the country," some vacancies would unexpectedly arise during that recess due to resignation or death. The recess-appointment mechanism therefore intended to be a "supplement" to the normal advice-and-consent route when the public interest required that the post be filled forthright, the Heritage Foundation explained. The Supreme Court itself interpreted the provision in 2014. "Presidents have made recess appointments since the beginning of the Republic," the Court said in *National Labor Relations Board v. Noel Canning*. Amazingly, that was the first time the Court had cause to interpret the more than two-hundred-year-old clause. In *Noel Canning*, the Court detailed the "thousands of recess appointments reaching all the way back to the founding era." But the Court's *Noel Canning* decision seemed to foreclose the option of a recess appointment for Garland. The Senate was in session—and thus not in a recess—whenever the Senate said so, the Court unanimously held. It was extremely unlikely that the Senate would go into recess long enough to allow Obama to make a recess appointment.

Next, some liberals floated the idea of a procedural workaround that would bypass the Judiciary Committee and bring a vote to the Senate floor. That was a motion to discharge. Such a motion, though, ultimately proved to be unworkable. Democrats would eventually have to muster sixty votes to avoid a filibuster. At the time, they held only forty-six seats.

Some liberals hoping for a Democratic majority on the Supreme Court got desperate. One commentator said Obama should just appoint Garland to the bench and bypass the Senate altogether if the Senate refused to act. "It is altogether proper to view a decision by the Senate not to act as a waiver of its right to provide advice and consent," New York attorney Gregory L. Diskant said in a *Washington Post* op-ed. One problem with that proposal was that it was most likely unconstitutional. Because the advice-and-consent clause in the Constitution is so ambiguous, it is not clear exactly what role the Founders envisioned for the Senate. The meaning of the clause, therefore, has been derived "largely by historical traditions and practices," Winkler said, then continued, "There is no historical tradition for forcing a nominee onto the Supreme Court against the Senate's will."

More importantly, though, attempting such gimmicks to get Garland confirmed threatened the legitimacy of not only Judge Garland but also the Supreme Court itself. The more the Court became embroiled in politics, the greater the risk that all of its decisions would be seen as illegitimate, Counsel to the President Neil Eggleston said at a *Politico* event. That was why it was enormously important that the president "play it straight" with Garland's nomination, he said. And waiting did not seem to be that risky. If Donald Trump were to win the Republican nomination, Democrats would be in a strong position to win the presidency, Ilya Somin, a respected libertarian-leaning professor, told me while I was covering the vacancy for *Bloomberg BNA*. Moreover, Republicans could lose a number of seats in the Senate with such an unpopular presidential candidate on the ballot. At that point, Obama could easily get Garland—or anyone else—confirmed, Somin suggested.

So Democrats and Republicans marched on, invoking their respective talking points. As a result, the Supreme Court, for the first time in a long time, became a political flash point in upcoming presidential and senatorial elections. Usually, the Supreme Court only factors in as a background issue in presidential elections. For example, only 7 percent of voters nationwide identified the Supreme Court as the most important factor in their decision to vote following the 2008 presidential election, according to an *NBC News* exit poll. In the 2016 election, 22 percent of voters said the Supreme Court topped their list of election-day considerations. Not only was that increase in importance felt in the presidential election, it also played out in the thirty-four senatorial races that took place in 2016. The public argument between those who supported confirmation hearings for Garland and those who did not helped educate the public about not only the president's role in seating a Supreme Court justice but the Senate's role as well, political science professor Mark C. Miller explained. He pointed to a political ad funded by Planned Parenthood that targeted New Hampshire Republican

Senator Kelly Ayotte. The ad took aim at her opposition to holding confirmation hearings for Garland. At the time, Ayotte was running in a tight race against the state's Democratic governor Maggie Hassan. The race was seen as a harbinger of whether the 115th Senate would be run by Democrats or Republicans. Republicans ultimately held onto control of the Senate, but Ayotte lost her seat to Hassan. In a strange twist of fate, while her decision to support delaying Supreme Court confirmation hearings for Garland likely contributed to her loss, Ayotte would eventually be tapped to shepherd President Donald Trump's nominee to succeed Justice Scalia, Judge Neil Gorsuch, through his confirmation battle.

Both major party candidates made the Supreme Court a central focus of their platforms. Donald Trump released two lists of prominent conservative thinkers from which he pledged to pick if given the chance to fill the Scalia vacancy—a campaign promise that he kept early on in his presidency. The list was packed with young, influential federal appellate judges and state supreme court justices that would be sure to influence the trajectory of American legal thought for decades to come. The move was seen as an effort to convince conservative religious groups that Trump would appoint someone committed to overturning the right to an abortion affirmed in the Supreme Court's landmark decision *Roe v. Wade*. In fact, during the third and final presidential debate in October, Trump promised to appoint a justice who would "automatically" overturn *Roe v. Wade*. Many conservatives did indeed "hold their noses" and vote for Trump for this reason, despite serious concerns about his commitment to religious values and lack of respect for women.

Hillary Clinton too tried to use the Supreme Court vacancy to attract voters that otherwise might stay home or vote for a more progressive candidate. One problem for Clinton, professor Miller told me, was that supporters of surprisingly potent primary challenger Vermont Senator Bernie Sanders were not particularly excited by Merrick Garland. Garland was white. He was male. He was old by modern Supreme Court nominee standards, meaning that his potential impact on the Court would be limited. The previous eight justices confirmed to the Court ranged in age from forty-three (Justice Clarence Thomas) to sixty (Justice Ruth Bader Ginsburg). Garland was sixty-three when Obama nominated him to succeed Scalia. That lack of enthusiasm may be why Clinton did not refer very often to Garland during the election, though she often spoke of the vacancy in general. When the issue came up during the presidential debates, Clinton said she hoped "the Senate would do its job and confirm the nominee." She did not, however, refer to Garland by name, noted *SCOTUSblog*'s Amy Howe: "Clinton did not say, and [the moderator] did not ask, whether she would re-nominate Garland if she were elected and the Senate had not acted on his nomination by the time she took office."

In striking contrast to the attention that the presidential candidates gave to the Supreme Court vacancy was the indifferent way the justices themselves treated it—at least publicly. Just a week and a half after Justice Scalia's death, his ten-year colleague Justice Alito said the Supreme Court would manage without a full bench. "We will deal with it," Alito said, according to CNN's Ariane de Vogue. He said Scalia's death had come as a "great shock" to the justices, known for their collegiality despite their occasional vigorous and public disputes. But Alito said the Court was starting to get back to business, de Vogue recalled.

The justices did not even passingly mention the then current Supreme Court vacancy when considering a case that was solely about vacancies and the importance of the Senate's advice-and-consent duties. The question in *National Labor Relations Board v. Southwest General, Inc.* centered on the interpretation of the Federal Vacancies Reform Act (FVRA). The statute details who the president can tap to fill so-called PAS positions—those that require both presidential appointment and Senate confirmation—temporarily (as an "acting" official) while the Senate considers the president's nominee.

For decades prior to the enactment of the FVRA, presidents on both sides of the aisle used these acting positions as a way to circumvent the Senate if it refused to confirm the president's preferred nominee. "These acting officers filled high-level positions, sometimes in obvious contravention of the Senate's wishes," the Supreme Court explained in *Southwest General* in an opinion by the chief justice. The "turning point," as Justice Sotomayor put it in her dissenting opinion, was Bill Lann Lee. Lee "was brought in from outside Government to serve as Acting Assistant Attorney General for the Civil Rights Division of the Justice Department, immediately after the Senate refused to confirm him for that very office," the Supreme Court explained. He led the powerful Civil Rights Division for two and a half years in this acting capacity, despite the fact that he was never confirmed by the Senate. In response to these kinds of shenanigans, Congress passed the FVRA, which required that certain acting officials step down if nominated to fill the post permanently. The question for the justices in *Southwest General* was which acting officials that applied to. Ultimately, the Supreme Court interpreted the requirement broadly in a decision that split the Court 6–2.

Remarkably, in the one hour of oral argument in the case and the thirty-nine pages of the Court's majority, concurring, and dissenting opinions, not once did the justices note the extended vacancy that they were enduring on the Court itself. The majority described the Senate's advice-and-consent power as "a critical structural safeguard. . . . The constitutional process of Presidential appointment and Senate confirmation, however, can take time: The President may not promptly settle on a nominee to fill an office; the Senate may be unable, or unwilling, to speedily confirm the nominee once submitted. Yet neither may desire to see the duties of the vacant office go unperformed in the interim." As pregnant as those words may seem in the context of the fight over Garland's confirmation, the Court refused to say anything explicit about its application to the ongoing controversy and chose instead merely to go about its business without official comment.

Justice Neil Gorsuch was confirmed by the Republican-led Senate 67 days after President Trump nominated him to the high court bench. Intriguingly, that was the average number of days from nomination to confirmation of a modern Supreme Court justice, according to Brian Deese, an Obama senior advisor. Prior to Garland's nomination, the longest in modern history was 125 days. That was for the renowned Justice Louis Brandeis. Judge Garland's nomination expired on January 3, 2017, the day the new 115th Congress convened for its two-year session. It had been 294 days since President Obama had tapped him to be the next associate justice of the Supreme Court.

Upon his nomination to the Supreme Court, then Judge Gorsuch's first call was reported to be to Chief Judge Garland. Word of that classy gesture endeared many spectators to the soon-to-be justice, which certainly did not hurt his confirmation prospects. But the outcome was never really in doubt, despite considerable resentment on the part of the minority party. As Democratic Senator Jeff Merkley put it, for a long time to come, Gorsuch would be considered a man occupying a "stolen seat."

Chapter 3

Stand Idly By

Gorsuch's confirmation did not occur until near the end of the Supreme Court's 2016 term, leaving the court with just eight justices for the first six months of its nine-month term. One of the first mechanisms the shorthanded Court seemed to employ in combating the image of a political court was to avoid controversial cases like *Gloucester County v. G. G.* But before Justice Scalia's death during the previous term, the Court had already agreed to take cases that could prove divisive. Unable to find an escape hatch like that in *Gloucester County*, the Court took a different approach: delay.

The Supreme Court's terms run from October to June. From October to April, the Supreme Court hears oral arguments, alternating between roughly two weeks of arguments and two-week recesses during which the justices write their opinions. In each case that the Supreme Court hears—that is, where the Supreme Court grants certiorari—there are at least three rounds of "briefing": The party that asked the Supreme Court to look at the case, the petitioner, will file their opening brief. The opposing party will file a response, and the petitioner will get a chance to itself respond in a reply brief. All of this takes time. As such, only those cases that are granted cert before mid-January will be heard by the Court that same term. The remaining cases, absent special circumstances, will be heard in the Court's next term.

Interestingly, three cases that met that mid-January timeline for the 2015 term were not scheduled for argument. All three cases involved potentially divisive issues that threatened to split the even-numbered Court 4–4. One of those cases was *Trinity Lutheran Church of Columbia v. Comer*. Since the late 1800s, the state of Missouri has strictly prohibited funding to any religious organization. "[N]o money shall ever be taken from the public treasury, directly or indirectly, in aid of any church, sect or denomination of religion," Missouri's constitution states. The state has "a long history of maintaining a very high wall between church and state," said the intermediate federal court that considered the dispute before it reached the Supreme Court. Moreover, the Missouri Supreme Court has consistently upheld such barriers and enforced the state's Establishment Clause as "not only more explicit but more restrictive" than the federal one.

With this background, the Missouri Department of Natural Resources refused to allow Trinity Lutheran Church of Columbia to participate in its Playground Scrap Tire Surface Material grant program. Under that program, the department would provide funds to schools to resurface their playgrounds with recycled tires. The tires protected children from playground injuries and the use of old tires on the playground reduced their presence in garbage dumps. Two birds; one stone. Trinity Lutheran, which ran a licensed preschool, applied to receive a grant under the program. The church scored well in the ranking process, but it was nevertheless denied funds. The department argued that it was constitutionally forbidden from taking any money from the public treasury to aid a church. So Trinity Lutheran sued the state in January 2013, asserting that the state had unconstitutionally discriminated against it for no other reason than that it was a church. After suffering losses in both the district court and the intermediate appellate court, Trinity Lutheran's case reached the Supreme Court in November 2015. The Supreme Court quickly agreed to hear the case, granting Trinity Lutheran's petition for certiorari on January 15, 2016. A month later, Justice Scalia died.

The cert in *Trinity Lutheran* happened just in time to get in all the briefings before the Court stopped hearing oral arguments for the term. But the case did not appear on the expected April calendar, the last month the Court typically hears oral arguments. The Court has room to hear about a dozen cases each month. In April 2016, the Court heard only ten. So there was room on the calendar. Moreover, other cases that were granted cert on the same day as *Trinity Lutheran* had made the April calendar, including most notably the case involving the fraud conviction of disgraced former Virginia governor Bob McDonnell. In that case, the Supreme Court heard arguments on April 27, 2016, and unanimously reversed the governor's conviction on June 27, 2016, the last day of the term.

But Trinity Lutheran, along with two other parties who had brought their cases before the justices, was kept waiting. The next chance for the church's case to be heard would be in October. When the Court released its

October calendar, though, *Trinity Lutheran* again was not on the list. Same for November. Same for December. Same for January, February, and March. The case was finally set for argument on April 19. With Justice Gorsuch sworn in just nine days earlier, there would be nine justices on the bench to hear the case and therefore no possibility of an evenly split Court.

For the three terms stretching from October 2013 to June 2016, the average time from when the Supreme Court agreed to hear a case to when it set the case for oral argument varied from 145 days to 159, according to *SCOTUSblog*. For Trinity Lutheran, it was almost 400 days. Some court watchers suspected that the Court was hoping to get a ninth justice before it took on such divisive issues that could split them evenly. Each of the three cases postponed in this manner by the Supreme Court involved historically divisive subjects for the Supreme Court, said Peter Stris, who eventually argued for one of the parties in these three cases. Stris's cases involved class actions, a subject that nonlawyers may be surprised to learn has bitterly split the Roberts Court. Another case involved the Constitution's controversial Takings Clause, under which the government can take private property for certain governmental purposes. *Trinity Lutheran* too involved a contentious issue: religious liberty.

The Court had recently split 5–4 in two high-profile cases touching on religion. In 2014, it sided with religious groups seeking an exemption from the requirement of the Affordable Care Act mandating that employers provide workers with free contraceptive coverage. In *Burwell v. Hobby Lobby*, the Court split 5–4, finding that closely held corporations were entitled to an exemption if providing contraceptives violated the owners' sincerely held religious convictions. Specifically, the business owners objected to paying for their employees to access certain contraceptive methods that they considered abortifacients. The contraceptive mandate, as it was known, substantially burdened the owners' religious beliefs, the Supreme Court concluded in an opinion by Justice Alito. The government could not do that under the protective Religious Freedom Restoration Act (RFRA). Introduced in 1993 by then representative Chuck Schumer, who is now the Senate minority leader, the act was a response to a Supreme Court decision, *Employment Div., Dept. of Human Resources of Ore. v. Smith*, which permitted greater restrictions on religious exercise. The act passed the Senate 97–3. Guarding against religious exercise more robustly than the US Constitution, the act required that the government show that the burden on religion was necessary to achieve a compelling government interest. The government's interest in providing contraceptive care to women did not meet that demanding test because there were other ways the government could fulfill its goals without burdening religious practice, the Supreme Court said in the *Hobby Lobby* case.

The decision provoked a stinging dissent from Justice Ginsburg, joined by her three liberal colleagues. "In a decision of startling breadth, the Court holds that commercial enterprises, including corporations, along with partnerships and sole proprietorships, can opt out of any law (saving only tax laws) they judge incompatible with their sincerely held religious beliefs," Ginsburg said in the first sentence of her opinion. "Would the exemption the Court holds RFRA demands for employers with religiously grounded objections to the use of certain contraceptives extend to employers with religiously grounded objections to blood transfusions (Jehovah's Witnesses); antidepressants (Scientologists); medications derived from pigs, including anesthesia, intravenous fluids, and pills coated with gelatin (certain Muslims, Jews, and Hindus); and vaccinations (Christian Scientists, among others)? . . . Persuaded that Congress enacted RFRA to serve a far less radical purpose, and mindful of the havoc the Court's judgment can introduce, I dissent," Ginsburg said. Notably, justices will often say that they "respectfully dissent" with their colleagues' decisions. Ginsburg did not.

But language of respect did appear earlier that year in *Town of Greece v. Galloway*, another notable case touching on religion. There, the Court considered an Upstate New York town's policy of inviting clergyman to offer prayers before the town's monthly board meetings. From 1999 to 2007, all of those clergymen were Christian. Two non-Christian citizens challenged the practice, claiming that it violated the First Amendment's Establishment Clause, preventing the government from favoring one religion over another. These prayers had to be "nonsectarian," the citizens argued.

The Supreme Court disagreed. The town's prayer practice fit "within the tradition long followed in Congress and the state legislatures," the Supreme Court said in an opinion authored by swing Justice Kennedy. "From the earliest days of the Nation, these [sectarian] invocations have been addressed to assemblies comprising many different creeds," Kennedy said. "These ceremonial prayers strive for the idea that people of many faiths may be united in a community of tolerance and devotion. Even those who disagree as to religious doctrine may find common ground in the desire to show respect for the divine in all aspects of their lives and being," he continued. "Our tradition assumes that adult citizens, firm in their own beliefs, can tolerate and perhaps appreciate a ceremonial prayer delivered by a person of a different faith."

Justice Kagan, in an opinion joined by her three liberal colleagues, "respectfully" dissented. The Constitution mandates "religious equality—the breathtakingly generous constitutional idea that our public institutions belong no less to the Buddhist or Hindu than to the Methodist or Episcopalian," Kagan said. The Constitution does not require the nonsectarian invocations the challengers were claiming, but the town's practice here "crossed a constitutional line," she suggested. By inviting only Christian clergy to lead these prayers month in and month out, the town "aligned itself with, and placed its imprimatur on, a particular religious creed," Kagan said. In doing so, the town "betrayed" its constitutional promise to its citizens, she said.

Trinity Lutheran came to the Supreme Court against this backdrop. Religious questions touching on hotly contested issues had recently put the Supreme Court in the limelight. So it was no wonder observers speculated that the Court wanted to avoid deciding such an issue while the spotlight was trained on the Court as the result of the openly political battle between Republicans and Democrats in the Senate.

That concern, however, did not bear out. On the Court's final day of the 2016 term, it handed down its decision in *Trinity Lutheran*. It was 7–2. Democrat-appointed justices Breyer and Kagan had sided with their conservative colleagues in deciding that Missouri had violated

Trinity Lutheran's free exercise rights by discriminating against it solely on the basis of its status as a religious institution. The Establishment Clause prohibits the government from favoring a particular religion. But the Free Exercise Clause allows individuals to practice their religion free from government interference. Taken to "a logical extreme," each of the clauses "tend[s] to clash with the other," Justice Sotomayor explained in dissent. But that did not happen here, the majority argued. The federal Establishment Clause does not prohibit the payments of the Missouri resurfacing program because providing Trinity Lutheran with a "generally available benefit" did not favor the church's specific religion, the chief declared in his opinion for the Court. So there was no Establishment Clause concern here. On the other hand, Missouri's policy put "Trinity Lutheran to a choice: It may participate in an otherwise available benefit program or remain a religious institution," the Court said. Requiring a religious group to "disavow its religious character" in order to obtain a generally available benefit impinged on the group's religious exercise.

While the Supreme Court may have miscalculated the divisiveness of *Trinity Lutheran*, the Court's 2016 term was rife with examples of the justices batting away controversial issues that threatened to bring the Court even more into the limelight. Two such cases—one out of Texas, the other out of North Carolina—involved changes to voting requirements.

In 2011, the Texas legislature passed—on an expedited basis—Senate Bill 14 (SB 14), which required that voters present one of a few accepted forms of identification before voting. Legislators said the law was necessary to combat voter fraud. Nevertheless, the law did not go into effect because the Voting Rights Act (VRA) required that any voting changes in Texas first be approved by federal officials, a process known as "preclearance." Preclearance required the approval of either the attorney general or a three-judge federal court sitting in Washington, DC. SB 14 failed to get approval from either.

In 2013, however, the Supreme Court released Texas and most other jurisdictions required to gain preclearance from the Voting Rights Act's requirements. The "coverage formula" that Congress used to determine which states and counties were subject to preclearance had not been updated since 1975. As a result, coverage was "based on decades-old data and eradicated practices," the Supreme Court said in *Shelby County v. Holder*. Congress could not do that, the Supreme Court decided. Although the Court acknowledged that "any racial discrimination in voting is too much," it warned Congress that it "must ensure that the legislation it passes to remedy that problem speaks to current conditions."

Following the Court's decision in *Shelby County*, Texas began implementing SB 14. Several Texas voters challenged the law in federal court, claiming that it violated section 2 of the Voting Rights Act. That section prohibits changes in voting laws that would result "in a denial or abridgement of the right of any citizen of the United States to vote on account of race or color." Applicable nationwide, the Supreme Court had left section 2 intact in *Shelby County*.

A federal district court sitting in Texas held a nine-day trial in 2014. It agreed with the challengers that "SB 14 creates an unconstitutional burden on the right to vote."

Approximately "608,470 registered voters in Texas, representing approximately 4.5 percent of all registered voters," lacked the qualified IDs, the court said. "Moreover, a disproportionate number of African-Americans and Hispanics populate that group of potentially disenfranchised voters." As such, the law was unconstitutional because it had a discriminatory effect on minorities.

But the district court went further. "[The] proponents of SB 14 within the 82nd Texas Legislature were motivated, at the very least in part, *because of* and not merely *in spite of* the voter ID law's detrimental effects on the African-American and Hispanic electorate," the court said. The court based its determination regarding the intent behind SB 14 in part on the fact that Texas legislators rationalized the voter ID law as a way to combat in-person voter fraud. In the ten years prior to SB 14's enactment, though, "only two cases of in-person voter impersonation fraud were prosecuted to a conviction—a period of time in which 20 million votes were cast," the court described. It prohibited the state from enforcing the law in upcoming elections. The Fifth Circuit, which handles cases from Texas, Louisiana, and Mississippi, stayed that order while it considered the state's appeal. The challengers of the law twice asked the Supreme Court to step in and halt the Fifth Circuit's own stay. Both times, however, the high court refused.

The Fifth Circuit, considered one of the most conservative in the country, issued its decision on the merits of the case in 2016. While the vast majority of circuit court cases are considered by a three-judge panel, the Texas voter ID case was considered "en banc," a special procedure by which all active judges on the circuit, sometimes joined by semiretired "senior judges," will consider a case of sufficiently weighty importance. Circuit courts infrequently sit en banc. From September 2015 to September 2016, a total of 36,547 cases were resolved on the merits—meaning there was no procedural issue that derailed the case, according to the administrative offices of the US courts. Of those thousands of cases, only forty-one were resolved via an en banc court. So it is safe to say that the en banc procedure is generally reserved for the most significant cases.

That is exactly what Texas's voter ID case was. By a vote of 9–6, the Fifth Circuit agreed that SB 14 had an impermissible discriminatory effect on minorities. But the appellate court undid the district court's finding with regard to discriminatory intent. It noted that there was "evidence that could support a finding that the Legislature's race-neutral reason of ballot integrity offered by the State is pretextual." The evidence that the district court relied on to make such a determination, though, was "infirm." As such, the Fifth Circuit sent the case back to the district court to consider the intent behind SB 14 again.

The six judges who wanted to uphold the voter ID law started their opinion simply enough: "We dissent." What followed, though, was a fiery rebuke of what they called the "ill-conceived, misguided, and unsupported majority." In an opinion by former chief judge Edith Jones, the dissenters said, "Requiring a voter to verify her identity with a photo ID at the polling place is a reasonable requirement widely supported by Texans of all races and members of the public belonging to both political parties." By keeping alive the discriminatory intent claim, "the majority fans the flames of perniciously irresponsible racial name-calling." Likening the majority to "Area 51 alien enthusiasts who, lacking any real evidence, espied a vast but clandestine government conspiracy to conceal the 'truth,'" the dissenters challenged the majority to have the "courage to distinguish between invidious motivation and shadows."

Armed with that brutal dissent, Texas asked the Supreme Court to consider the case for itself. The request was meaningfully different from the requests the law's challengers previously made to the Supreme Court. Their previous requests asked the justices to halt SB 14's enforcement, even though the Fifth Circuit had allowed it to remain in place while the lower court considered the state's appeal. In ruling on those stay requests, one consideration the justices would have taken into account was the institutional preference to preserve the status quo while the case worked its way through the court system. With regard to SB 14, the status quo was to allow the law to remain in place. But Texas's request now asked the Supreme Court not merely to pause the case while the lower courts decided but to make the decision itself. True, the justices only agree to hear about seventy cases each term, so it was by no means a foregone conclusion that the Supreme Court would agree to hear Texas's case. One factor that *relatively* frequently tips the balance is when a federal court strikes down a state law. Such actions raise important concerns with regard to federalism and separation of powers. And that was exactly what had happened with SB 14. Yet on January 23, 2017, the Supreme Court turned the case away. The justices' votes on whether to hear a case are done in a closed-door conference. Justices who find themselves on the losing end of such a determination can choose whether to publicly note their dissent. But there was no noted dissent in the Texas case.

There was, however, a curious "statement respecting the denial of certiorari" from the chief justice. Texas "asks the Court to review whether the Texas Legislature enacted SB14 with a discriminatory purpose and whether the law results in a denial or abridgment of the right to vote under §2," the chief said. He stressed that there was "no barrier" to the Court's review. Nevertheless, the case was not ready for Supreme Court to weigh in, pointing to the fact that the district court was charged with reconsidering the discriminatory-intent claim. Once the district court enters a final judgment on that and other outstanding issues, the case "will be better suited for certiorari review at that time," the chief said. In other words, not right now.

The chief justice's statement would come to mind nearly five months later, when the Court similarly turned away a voter ID case out of North Carolina. Like Texas, North Carolina had passed its own voter ID law in the wake of the Supreme Court's *Shelby County* decision. North Carolina's law, however, was combined with a number of other voting changes. The law reduced the number of "early voting" days from seventeen to ten. It dismantled out-of-precinct voting—the ability to have your vote count even if cast in the wrong place. It eliminated same-day registrations—enabling a voter to register and vote on the same day. Finally, it turned away sixteen- and seventeen-year-olds who wanted to "pre-register" to vote. "Each modified or removed voting and registration mechanism was enacted while Democrats controlled both houses of North Carolina's General Assembly and its governorship," the district court observed. "Some of these measures were controversial when enacted, and one—out-of-precinct provisional voting—was passed on a purely partisan basis in a manner designed to gain Democrats electoral victory retroactively." In finding that the now-in-control Republicans could constitutionally rein in those Democratic policies, the district court pointed out that many states, including New York, currently did not allow same-day registration or liberal use of absentee voting. If some states could refuse to allow such procedures altogether, it was not clear why North Carolina could not "retrench" those policies, the court suggested.

The district court ultimately upheld North Carolina's law. In doing so, it detailed its "monumental challenge" in coming to that conclusion. The court had to battle with a record of more than twenty-five thousand pages. It held a four-day evidentiary hearing and more than twenty-one days of trial. And it reviewed the testimony of 133 witnesses in total.

The challengers of the law appealed to the Fourth Circuit, the same circuit that had ruled in favor of Grimm in his meandering bid for transgender rights. The markedly courteous Fourth Circuit, which is based in Richmond, Virginia, was once considered one of the nation's most conservative courts. But it, like many of the thirteen federal appellate courts, swung decidedly to the left under President Obama, who—like many presidents—was able to appoint nearly half of the federal bench during his presidency. "When President Barack Obama took office on Inauguration Day 2009, only five of the 4th Circuit's 15 judgeships were filled by Democratic appointees," according to Josh Siegel of the conservative online publication,

The Daily Signal. By June 2017, the Fourth Circuit had "a higher percentage of Democratic appointees than even the San Francisco–based 9th Circuit, a court with a liberal reputation," Siegel said. By the time Obama left office, Democratic presidents had appointed ten of the court's fifteen judges.

Such was the state of the Fourth Circuit when it heard the challenge to North Carolina's voter ID law. It commended the district court for its "thoroughness." However, by "holding that the legislature did not enact the challenged provisions with discriminatory intent, the court seems to have missed the forest in carefully surveying the many trees," the Fourth Circuit chided. The state offered "only meager justifications" for the necessity of such restrictive voting measures. "Although the new provisions target African Americans with almost surgical precision, they constitute inapt remedies for the problems assertedly justifying them and, in fact, impose cures for problems that did not exist." The state legislature's "true motivation" was to curtail minority voters' ability to vote because they were "about to exercise it." That "bears the mark of intentional discrimination," the Fourth Circuit said, striking down the law.

The case came to the Supreme Court in late December 2016. Cases generally must be appealed to the Supreme Court within ninety days of the lower court's ruling. With the Fourth Circuit ruling against North Carolina in late July 2016, the state's request for Supreme Court's review was due before the gubernatorial elections. But the state petitioned for, and got, an extension to file its request after the November elections. That was quite possibly a consequential request. North Carolina finally filed its request for Supreme Court review on December 27. Before that, however, Democratic candidate Roy Cooper overtook Republican incumbent Pat McCrory in the governor's race. Former state attorney general Cooper was replaced by Democrat Josh Stein. Incredibly, though Republicans have been twice appointed to the post, a Republican has not won a race for attorney general in North Carolina since 1897.

With Democrats now holding considerably more power in the state, they sought to withdraw their appeal in February 2017. "We need to make it easier for people to exercise their right to vote, not harder, and I will not continue to waste time and money appealing this unconstitutional law," Cooper said. The state's general assembly balked. Only it had the power to press or withdraw claims in courts, the general assembly told the Supreme Court. The new governor's attempt to withdraw the case at this late stage was "nothing less than a politically-motivated attempt to hijack a certiorari petition in a major Voting Rights Act case." The Supreme Court decided to stay out of the local spat. It refused to review the Fourth Circuit's decision on May 15, 2017.

Again, however, there was a peculiar "statement" from the chief: "Given the blizzard of filings over who is and who is not authorized to seek review in this Court under North Carolina law, it is important to recall our frequent admonition that '[t]he denial of a writ of certiorari imports no expression of opinion upon the merits of the case.'" In other words, we are not going to look at this case ourselves, but that does not mean we agree with the outcome.

Both the North Carolina and Texas voter ID cases demonstrate that voter identification and other restrictive voting measures are controversial and politically divisive. In the Texas case, the conservative Fifth Circuit overturned perhaps the most consequential part of the district court's complete invalidation of the state's voter ID law. In the North Carolina case, the now liberal Fourth Circuit did a complete 180-degree turn on the district court's blessing of the state's voting law. But the Supreme Court, once again, managed to remain above the fray.

Similar maneuvering by the Court in a gun rights case, though, provoked the ire of Justice Thomas, long considered the Roberts Court's most conservative member. The issue at the heart of *Peruta v. California* was a state concealed-carry law. Such laws determine when an applicant is allowed to carry a concealed firearm in public. The overwhelming majority of states are "shall-issue" states, meaning that the state has little discretion in issuing such permits. In these places, "a law-abiding person shall be granted a permit to carry concealed firearms" upon completion of certain requirements, according to the National Rifle Association's (NRA) Institute for Legislative Action. Indeed, twelve states require no permit at all to carry a concealed firearm. But eight states are considered "may-issue." In these jurisdictions, the government is given "complete discretion over the issuance of carry permits," the NRA says. Officials may issue concealed-carry permits, but they are not required to—and they often do not.

California is among the minority of states that has one of these may-issue regimes. The state has a number of statutory prerequisites to obtaining a concealed-carry permit. Passing a criminal background check, completing a safety course, and proving a "good cause" to carry such a permit are among the statutory requirements. But the state delegates to the localities the power to define what "good cause" means.

Edward Peruta and other area residents applied for but were denied concealed-carry permits because they could not meet San Diego's definition of good cause. Good cause, the county policy said, was "a set of circumstances that distinguish the applicant from the mainstream and causes him or her to be placed in harm's way. Simply fearing for one's personal safety alone is not considered good cause." Instead, the applicant had to demonstrate that "they are a specific target at risk" by providing "documented threats, restraining orders, and other related situations." So Peruta and the other residents sued the county, arguing that such a stringent condition on the approval of a concealed-carry permit ran afoul of the Second Amendment's protection of the right to bear arms.

After a federal trial court initially upheld San Diego's restrictive policy, the case headed to the Ninth Circuit. The Ninth Circuit hears cases from California, eight other states, and two US territories. Due in large part to its jurisdiction over California, the Ninth Circuit is by far the largest of the thirteen federal appellate courts. Nearly 20 percent of the US population lives within the purview of this court. Of the nearly forty-three thousand appeals pending in all federal appellate courts at the end of 2016, more than thirteen thousand were in the Ninth Circuit.

The Ninth Circuit is also notoriously among those whose decisions are the most consistently overturned by the Supreme Court. Of the sixty-nine cases that the Supreme Court decided during its 2016 term, eight came from the Ninth Circuit. That court ended up with a record of 1–7, the second worst record among the courts reviewed by the Supreme Court. Arguably related is the fact that the Ninth Circuit is considered the most liberal of the thirteen federal appellate courts. As of January 2017, eighteen of the full-time "active" judges on that court were appointed by Democrats and seven by Republicans, according to the progressive American Constitution Society.

As mentioned previously, most appeals are considered by a panel consisting of three judges. Despite the lopsided number of Democratic appointees on the Ninth Circuit, the appellate panel in Peruta's case consisted of two judges appointed by Republican presidents and one by a Democrat. That panel concluded that San Diego's policy violated the Second Amendment right "of the people to keep and bear Arms." The victory was short-lived, though. An "en banc" Ninth Circuit court reversed course and upheld the law.

Though an en banc court typically includes all the active judges in the circuit, as well as any semiretired judges that sat on the original panel, this normally does not happen on the Ninth Circuit because it is so large. Instead, the Ninth Circuit's en banc court usually consists of the chief judge, ten randomly drawn judges, and any semiretired judge that was on the original panel, according to the Ninth Circuit's Public Information Office. Again, federal appellate courts do not often sit en banc, and the Ninth Circuit is no exception. Its Public Information Office noted that the Ninth Circuit considers some 1,550 en banc request each year, saying, "On the average, the Ninth Circuit hears between 15–25." *Peruta,* however, was one of the select few cases that the Ninth Circuit determined qualified for en banc consideration. The en banc court consisted of eight Democrat-appointed judges and three Republican-appointed ones. The decision upholding San Diego's policy was 7–4.

The case arrived at the Supreme Court in January 2017. It was first "distributed" for conference on March 24, meaning that the justices would discuss the case in their semiregular private meetings. During these private conferences, the justices consider whether to hear a particular case or to turn it away. But before the justices considered *Peruta* in conference, it was rescheduled. A single justice can request that a case be rescheduled and pushed off to another conference, but the court does not publicly note which justice requested the delay. The court's docket simply says "Rescheduled." The case was distributed for the next conference, but the day before that conference, it was again "Rescheduled." That happened two more times before *Peruta* finally made it before the justices on April 28, suggesting that at least one justice seemed to be looking closely into the case. There was no word about *Peruta* on the Court's next orders list, where the justices say whether they have or have not agreed to take up a case. That was a good sign as the Court typically "relists" a case before agreeing to hear it—that is, they will consider it at another conference to ensure that there are no procedural hiccups that could derail the Court's consideration of the case. But week after week, there was no word about what the Court would do with *Peruta*. At each of the Court's final eight conferences of the 2016 term, the justices presumably discussed the case. On the final day of the term, the justices finally revealed *Peruta*'s fate. "The petition for a writ of certiorari is denied," the order said in full.

Justice Thomas not only noted his dissent from the Court's refusal to hear the case; he also wrote an eight-page dissenting opinion laying out his disagreement with the Court's decision. He was joined by the newly minted Justice Gorsuch. The Ninth Circuit's decision upholding San Diego's policy was "indefensible," Thomas wrote. In arguing that the Supreme Court should reconsider that flawed decision, he pointed to one of Justice Scalia's most storied opinions, *District of Columbia v. Heller*. The 2008 *Heller* case was the first time since 1939 that the high court directly considered the scope of the Second Amendment. That irregularly worded amendment professes that "[a] well regulated militia, being necessary to the security of a free state, the right of the people to keep and bear arms shall not be infringed." In *Heller*, the Supreme Court found that the right to a firearm in one's home was not conditioned on militia service. The amendment also protected the right to a firearm in one's home for self-defense, the *Heller* decision said. Although *Heller* did not directly address the right to carry a firearm outside of the home—as was the issue in *Peruta*—the case nevertheless compelled that conclusion, Thomas argued. "As we explained in *Heller*, to 'bear arms' means to 'wear, bear, or carry upon the person or in the clothing or in a pocket, for the purpose of being armed and ready for offensive or defensive action in a case of conflict with another person,'" Thomas said. "The most natural reading of this definition encompasses public carry. I find it extremely improbable that the Framers understood the Second Amendment to protect little more than carrying a gun from the bedroom to the kitchen."

But even if his colleagues did not agree, Thomas said it was time for the Supreme Court to provide a definitive answer. "Twenty-six States have asked us to resolve the question presented," Thomas said, referring to an amicus brief filed by several states. "At least four other Courts of Appeals and three state courts of last resort have decided cases regarding the ability of States to regulate the public carry of firearms. Those decisions (plus the one below) have produced thorough opinions on both sides of the issue." Thomas, therefore, did not "see much value in waiting."

Thomas then really took his colleagues to task. "The Court's decision to deny certiorari in this case reflects a distressing trend: the treatment of the Second Amendment as a disfavored right. . . . [But the] Constitution does not rank certain rights above others, and I do not think this Court should impose such a hierarchy by selectively enforcing its preferred rights," he said. "The Court has not heard argument in a Second Amendment case in over seven years." In that time, the Court had "heard argument in, for example, roughly 35 cases where the question presented turned on the meaning of the First Amendment and 25 cases that turned on the meaning of the Fourth Amendment. This discrepancy is inexcusable, especially given how much less developed our jurisprudence is with respect to the Second Amendment as compared to the First and Fourth Amendments." Thomas concluded with the following: "For those of us who work in marbled halls, guarded constantly by a vigilant and dedicated police force, the guarantees of the Second Amendment might seem antiquated and superfluous. But the Framers made a clear choice: They reserved to all Americans the right to bear arms for self-defense. I do not think we should stand by idly while a State denies its citizens that right, particularly when their very lives may depend on it. I respectfully dissent."

Chapter 4

Quarter-Loaf Outcomes

The Supreme Court's desire to stay out of controversial cases in order to duck the limelight and avoid evenly split decisions led to a light docket filled with relatively inconsequential cases. Indeed, the term's sixty-nine decisions was a historically low number, as the Court issued fewer decisions in the 2016 term than it had since the mid-1880s, according to Adam Feldman, creator of *Empirical SCOTUS*. Although more acute this term, the decline in the Court's caseload was not new. In a moment of levity during one of the term's particularly dull cases, *Lightfoot v. Cendant Mortgage*, Chief Justice Roberts asked an arguing attorney to respond to the allegation that his position would add sixty thousand more cases to the federal judiciary's docket. "Don't tell us we're not working hard enough," Justice Kennedy quipped. "I do recall, Justice Kennedy, that once upon a time, the Court took 150 cases a year," the attorney countered. "They were easier cases," the chief joked.

The decrease in the Court's docket has been attributed to many things. But one notable factor seems to be the way in which the justices pick the cases that they will hear each term. The Court receives thousands of cert petitions each term. In the 1970s, to make the job of reviewing such petitions more efficient, Justice Lewis F. Powell Jr. floated the idea of a "cert pool," in which the justices divide the petitions among their chambers and distribute them to their clerks for initial review. The clerks draft memos summarizing the factual and legal issues in the case and make recommendations on whether to grant or deny cert. Forty years later, the cert pool is alive and thriving with all but two of the current justices participating. That gives enormous power to the justices' clerks—typically incredibly smart twenty-somethings with little life experience beyond school and clerking. "You stick your neck out as a clerk when you recommend to grant a case," Justice John Paul Stevens told *USA Today* in 1998. "The risk-averse thing to do is to recommend not to take a case. I think it accounts for the lessening of the docket," Stevens said.

The relatively few cases that the Supreme Court did decide during its 2016 term, however, garnered a remarkable amount of consensus. The justices recorded no dissent in more than half of the cases it decided during the 2016 term, marking only the second time in modern Supreme Court history that the number of unanimous decisions outpaced nonunanimous ones, according to Feldman. The justices were able to unanimously agree on the outcome of a billion-dollar intellectual property fight between tech giants Samsung and Apple. They unanimously ruled against an American corporation in its suit against Venezuela for nationalizing oil rigs owned by one of its subsidiaries. And the Court was able to reach consensus in cases dealing with issues as wide-ranging as the criminal penalties against an unlikely meth conspirator and a procedural quirk in patent law.

The latter case involved "venue," which in legal circles refers to the proper court (or courts) in which a defendant can be sued. There is both a general venue statute and one that governs patent cases specifically. In 1957, the Supreme Court considered the patent-specific statute designating the proper place to sue an alleged patent infringer. Taking a limited view of the statute, the Court said such defendants could only be sued in the state of their incorporation—that is, the state where the company came into existence and whose laws governed the company's fundamental operations. In the sixty years since the Court's decision, Congress amended the general statute governing where plaintiffs should sue defendants. As a result of those amendments, the generally applicable venue rules are much broader than the patent-specific one. Pertinently, the general venue rules allow plaintiffs to sue defendants anywhere they were harmed.

The question in *TC Heartland LLC v. Kraft Foods Group Brands LLC* was whether the amendments to the general venue rule affected the patent-specific one. Patent-specific rules are not unusual in the legal world. Most prominently, all appeals in patent cases are funneled to a special court, the Federal Circuit. Unlike the other federal circuit courts, the Federal Circuit's jurisdiction is not established via a geographical method. Only special cases go to the Federal Circuit, like those involving federal employees and those relating to international trade.

Nearly twenty years ago, the Federal Circuit decided that amendments to the general venue statute affected the patent-specific statute too. That decision drastically expanded where alleged patent infringers—frequently large businesses—could be sued. Because large businesses often sell their products nationwide, a patent holder claiming that those products infringe their patent—thereby causing the patent holder harm—could now sue the alleged infringer nationwide.

A trove of big businesses urged the Supreme Court to cut back on this broad view of venue. Walmart, FedEx, eBay, Intel, Dell, HP, Macy's, L.L.Bean, Overstock.com, QVC, and even Bass Pro Shops all weighed in in favor of a more restricted view. One of the most compelling amicus briefs came from General Electric. The iconic American conglomerate "holds thousands of U.S. patents and files for thousands of additional patents each year," it told the justices. The Federal Circuit's broad venue rulings have had a "significant and unfair impact on defendants accused of patent infringement." The broad rules had led to a concentration of patent cases filed in plaintiff-friendly courts. In 2015, more than 40 percent of all patent cases nationwide were filed in just one federal district, the Eastern District of Texas, GE pointed out. One of the courts in the Eastern District is located in Marshall, Texas, a town with a population of just under twenty-five thousand. Partly because that court has adopted rules perceived to be more favorable to patent plaintiffs, most of the patent cases filed in the Eastern District are filed there. The town's economy has seen a boom since the creation of the cottage industry. Hotels, restaurants, and other services have popped up to accommodate the glut of attorneys who visit the town to litigate their cases. A patent dispute over flavored drink mixes—that, oddly enough, was not filed in the Eastern District of Texas—threatened to significantly curb the boom local businesses saw as a result of so much litigation being filtered through the town.

And that very well could be what happens as a result of the Supreme Court's ultimate decision in *TC Heartland*. In an 8–0 opinion in which no other justice felt compelled to write a separate decision—either concurring or dissenting—the Court reversed the Federal Circuit's opinion. Its earlier decision had "definitively and unambiguously" limited the places that potential patent infringers could be sued to their place of incorporation, the Supreme Court said, in an opinion by Justice Thomas. In one way, the Supreme Court decision to reverse the Federal Circuit was not surprising. Like the Ninth Circuit, the Federal Circuit has, for a long time, tallied an abysmal record before the high court. During the 2016 term, the Federal Circuit went just 1–6, receiving only ten votes in its favor out of the fifty-six cast in those seven cases, according to *SCOTUSblog*'s statistics.

In another way, though, the Supreme Court's decision was a surprise. The Federal Circuit is notorious for divining unique rules that apply only to patent cases. The idea that such complex and specialized cases might not follow the same rules as all other cases churning through the federal courts is not outrageous. But the Supreme Court has emphatically rejected that individualized view of patent law. In *TC Heartland*, the Federal Circuit construed the laws to apply similarly in patent cases as in every other federal case. Nevertheless, it was overturned by the high court. "The Federal Circuit can't win even when it decides that patent litigation should follow the well-developed rules of mainstream civil procedure," Columbia law professor Ronald Mann noted on *SCOTUSblog*.

The same unanimity managed by the justices in that case, potentially affecting billions of dollars of the US economy, was also present in a case involving around seventy thousand dollars. It all started when Terry Michael Honeycutt noticed "edgy looking folks" at the hardware store he worked in, which was owned by his brother. These wearisome characters regularly purchased Polar Pure, "an iodine-based water-purification product," the Supreme Court explained. Each "bottle of Polar Pure contained enough iodine to purify 500 gallons of water." Nevertheless, customers would often buy "as many as 12 bottles in a single transaction." The justices detailed, "Over a 3-year period, the store grossed roughly $400,000 from the sale of more than 20,000 bottles of Polar Pure." Concerned with these troublesome quantities, Honeycutt contacted his local police department. Law enforcement officers urged Honeycutt to stop selling the product, as Polar Pure could be used to manufacture methamphetamine.

Honeycutt decided to ignore that advice. As a result, the brothers were criminally convicted, with Honeycutt being sentenced to five years in prison. The Supreme Court was not asked to overturn that lengthy sentence. Instead, Honeycutt asked the Court to claw back a monetary penalty the government had secured against him. The government had sought the hundreds of thousands of dollars that the brothers had earned as a result of their "drug crimes." The government was able to get a large part of this figure from Honeycutt's brother, the owner of the hardware store.

And the government went after Honeycutt for the remainder. Honeycutt cried foul, claiming that he never actually received any of the proceeds of the illegal sales. He was only a salaried worker, Honeycutt argued. Any profits went solely to his brother. The Sixth Circuit did not agree, finding that Honeycutt could be liable for the remaining seventy thousand dollars.

The Supreme Court had no trouble reversing that determination. In yet another 8–0 decision, the Court said the government could not get those funds from Honeycutt because he had never even received them. Writing for the Court, Justice Sotomayor, as the justices are known to do, provided a damning analogy:

> Suppose a farmer masterminds a scheme to grow, harvest, and distribute marijuana on local college campuses. The mastermind recruits a college student to deliver packages and pays the student $300 each month from the distribution proceeds for his services. In one year, the mastermind earns $3 million. The student, meanwhile, earns $3,600. If [the government's legal theory is correct], the student would face a forfeiture judgment for the entire amount of the conspiracy's proceeds: $3 million. The student would be bound by that judgment even though he never personally acquired any proceeds beyond the $3,600.

Even where there was not unanimity among the justices during the 2016 term, there tended to be a great degree of consensus. Only ten cases had more than two justices in dissent. In those cases, a core group of justices continued to constitute the heart of the majority. Justice Kennedy is frequently regarded as the Court's swing justice in close and often consequential cases. But over the last few terms, Chief Justice Roberts and Justices Breyer and Kagan have joined Justice Kennedy as determinative votes. As a result, these four justices have been the most often in the majority—in overall cases and in divided cases too. This term, the chief and Justices Kennedy, Breyer, and Kagan voted together approximately 70 percent of the time.

In getting to that consensus, though, the justices came to some very limited conclusions during the 2016 term. Presumably, in seeking to find agreement among the shorthanded bench, the justices settled on narrow results that could garner a majority. Consider the potentially salacious case of *State Farm Fire & Casualty Co. v. United States ex rel. Rigsby*. It originated from Hurricane Katrina's tragic path through the southeastern United States in 2005. The Category 5 hurricane was at the time "the costliest and one of the five deadliest hurricanes to ever strike the United States," according to a 2011 report from the National Hurricane Center. Katrina's catastrophic toll was due in large part to the fact that the storm "struck a portion of the United States coastline along the northern Gulf of Mexico that is particularly vulnerable to storm surge, leading to loss of life and property damage of immense proportions." It is hard to determine the number of deaths attributable to Hurricane Katrina, but the report estimates that the storm claimed more than 1,800 lives. Along with the human loss, the total cost of damage from Katrina's high winds and devastating floods was $108 billion.

State Farm had issued thousands of insurance policies to homeowners protected by the storm. Along with considering and paying claims on its own policies, State Farm was also responsible for policies issued by the National Flood Insurance Program. Under this Federal Emergency Management Agency (FEMA)–backed arrangement, State Farm would determine whether damage relating to a particular claim was caused by wind (which State Farm would be responsible for paying) or water (which would be paid by the federal government). All told, the federal government paid more than $16.3 billion in nearly 168,000 claims as a result of Hurricane Katrina. But State Farm should have paid much of that money itself, a jury determined in a 2013 "bellwether trial."

Bellwether trials occur where numerous plaintiffs assert similar claims against like defendants. The parties will agree to accelerate one or a group of cases to trial to establish law and test theories for future cases. The bellwether trial for claims related to fraud in administering the National Flood Insurance Program involved a claim submitted by Thomas and Pamela McIntosh. State Farm determined that the McIntosh's home was destroyed by flood, not wind damage. The lawsuit claimed that the finding was fraudulent, causing the federal government to pay out money to the McIntoshes when State Farm was really the financially responsible party. But it was not the McIntoshes who were suing State Farm. Instead, it was two of the insurance giant's former employees: sisters Cori and Kerri Rigsby. The Rigsby sisters said that they had thousands of pages of evidence that State Farm had deliberately misrepresented the nature of the damage in assessing claims from Hurricane Katrina. The Rigsby sisters, therefore, filed a qui tam action on behalf of the United States.

Chapter 4

The qui tam action is a unique procedure under the False Claims Act that allows private citizens, known as relators, to sue alleged fraudsters on behalf of the federal government. That act prohibits individuals or businesses from submitting false claims for payment by the federal government. It encourages whistleblowers to protect the interests of the federal government by allowing successful relators to share in any money judgment won on behalf of the United States in the suit. The Rigsbys' suit was successful. A jury found that the damage to the McIntosh's home was due solely to wind damage. State Farm, therefore, had submitted a false claim when it determined that the claim should be paid under the National Flood Insurance Program instead of by State Farm itself. After imposing various fines, the court issued a judgment against State Farm for $758,250. In addition to nearly $3 million in attorneys' fees, the Rigsby sisters got 30 percent of the judgment, or $227,475.

The Supreme Court considered arguably the narrowest issue in this procedurally intriguing and factually infuriating case: whether a violation of the False Claims Act's "seal requirement" necessitates a court to dismiss a relator's action. The seal requirement basically mandates that the realtor keep the lawsuit secret until the federal government decides whether it wants to participate. At the government's request, the court required that the suit remain under seal for several months. Before the seal had been lifted, however, Dickie Scruggs, the Rigsbys' lawyer, disclosed the existence of the lawsuit to several news outlets. Instead of remaining secret, the fraud allegations were the subject of numerous high-profile news features, including one on *20/20*. It was not Scruggs's only misstep with the judicial system. He had come to fame in the 1990s by winning upward of $200 billion from tobacco companies. But while he was representing the Rigsbys, he was indicted for attempting to bribe a state judge. He eventually pleaded guilty to that and another similar bribery scheme and would serve several years in prison.

Scruggs, however, would be released from prison before the consequences of his actions were known to those he represented in the State Farm litigation. It was not until December 6, 2016, that the Supreme Court ruled in the Rigsbys' favor. After the devastating jury verdict in the bellwether case, State Farm argued that the judgment should nevertheless be thrown out because of Scruggs's violations of the seal requirement. Congress struck a careful balance in the False Claims Act, State Farm argued. It wanted to encourage private whistleblowing but also desired to preserve the government's ability to investigate and pursue frauds against it. The False Claims Act's technical provisions, like the seal requirement, helped ensure that balance. Anything other than a bright-line rule punishing willful violations of Congress's desire would only encourage purposeful violations in the future, State Farm said.

The Supreme Court unanimously disagreed. The False Claims Act does not mandate "so harsh a rule," Justice Kennedy wrote for the 8–0 Court. A district court may dismiss a case as a result of a willful violation of the seal requirement, the Court said, but it was not mandatory. It was up to the district court's discretion whether to punish the plaintiffs for their attorney's illegal activities. Moreover, the Court stressed that district courts were free to assess some other penalty on the plaintiffs and their attorney, like monetary penalties or attorney sanctions.

Chapter 4

A similarly narrow fate befell the potentially momentous insider-trading case, *Salman v. United States.* Insider trading—which prohibits company insiders and those to whom they give tips from trading securities on nonpublic information—is a notoriously murky area of law. In part, that is due to the fact that there are no federal statutes explicitly prohibiting insider trading. Instead, courts have inferred the prohibition based on other, broad antifraud provisions. It has therefore been largely left to the courts to say what is, and is not, prohibited. The Supreme Court's attempt to do just that in 1983 added more confusion to this area of law. In *Dirks v. SEC,* the Court declared that insider-trading liability turns on whether the person providing the insider information—the tipper—does so in order to obtain a "personal benefit." The Court, however, did not concretely say what that meant.

Nearly twenty-five years later, the Second Circuit—wherein many federal securities cases are adjudicated—took a narrow view of "personal benefit" in the context of leaks of insider information to family members and friends. That close relationship alone could not provide the personal benefit needed to impose insider trading liability, the Second Circuit said in *United States v. Newman.* Instead, the government had to show that the tipper intended to get some pecuniary or other valuable benefit. The decision was a significant loss for the federal government as it made it harder for the United States to prosecute business insiders. Given the significance of the case, observers were somewhat surprised when the Court refused to hear the *Newman* case in 2015.

Adding to this surprise was the fact that there existed a curious circuit split on the personal-benefit issue.

Prominent district judge Jed Rakoff, whose court is under the jurisdiction of the Second Circuit, was openly critical of the *Newman* decision. As a district court judge, however, he was nearly powerless to do anything about it. Or was he? Federal judges occasionally help out their sister courts by "sitting by designation" in courts that are severely shorthanded. The Ninth Circuit, as the busiest circuit, often fits that bill. That had led Rakoff to sit by designation on the Ninth Circuit in previous years, and he had agreed to do so again 2015. In a completely fortuitous turn of events, Rakoff was assigned to hear a Ninth Circuit insider-trading case presenting the same issue as *Newman*. That case was *Salman v. United States*. Writing for a unanimous panel of two other judges, Rakoff parted ways with his home circuit. The close relationship between family members and friends alone could support the basis for an insider-trading conviction, Rakoff argued.

Although the peculiar circuit split was already in place when the Supreme Court refused to hear the *Newman* case, the justices decided to resolve the split in *Salman* instead. Yet the Court seemed to go out of its way to decide as little as possible. The justices unanimously agreed that the Ninth Circuit's decision should be upheld. But the majority of justices decided only that the specific relationship at issue in *Salman*—brother to brother—provided a sufficient personal benefit to find Salman guilty, according to frequent Supreme Court litigator Paul Clement. He presumed that if the Court had tried to go any further than that, the decision would not have been unanimous.

Bank of America v. Miami provides yet another example of the Court's narrow decision making during the term. The city sued banking giant Bank of America for discriminatory lending practices to African Americans and Latinos. Specifically, the city claimed that Bank of America violated the Fair Housing Act (FHA) by tricking minorities into agreeing to unfavorable lending terms. The question for the Supreme Court was not whether this was true but whether the city could even bring its claims in federal court. The city did not have "standing"—the legal authority to sue under a particular law—Bank of America argued. The Supreme Court disagreed . . . sort of. The city was an "aggrieved party" that could sue under the FHA, the Court decided, because the act allowed anyone injured by discriminatory lending practices to sue to enforce the act's provisions. Miami, the Court said, was injured because it alleged that the resulting foreclosures caused by the less favorable lending terms created blighted neighborhoods that forced the city "to spend more on municipal services to those communities, like increased police presence."

Yet the Court left undecided the question of whether the city had satisfied another prong of the standing analysis—namely, whether the city's alleged injuries were "proximately caused" by the bank's discriminatory lending or if the losses were instead fairly attributable to another cause. That was a question for the lower court to answer in the first instance, the Supreme Court claimed. By doing so, the Court merely shifted the fight from the aggrieved-party analysis to the proximate-cause one, Scott Nelson of the proconsumer group *Public Citizen* explained. This meant that the city would have to go back to the lower court and start all over again on a preliminary issue, meaning more time and energy spent on expensive litigation.

Nelson's frustration with the Court's narrow ruling was echoed by some of the justices themselves in *Expressions Hair Design v. Schneiderman*, a case that was oddly styled as a First Amendment case—oddly because what was at issue in *Expressions Hair Design* was a New York law forbidding store owners from charging a "surcharge" for the use of credit cards to cover the cost credit card companies charge to these stores for each credit card transaction. The challengers of the law said that the law impinged on their free speech rights because it would allow a shop to post a sign advertising a discount for paying with cash but would prohibit a similar sign describing an extra charge for a credit card purchase. Based on this framing of the case, the Supreme Court was asked to decide whether the law unconstitutionally prohibited speech based on the viewpoint being expressed. All eight justices agreed that the Court should undo the lower court's ruling upholding the law. But the majority of the justices reached that conclusion based on a very narrow ground. The law did regulate speech, the majority said, and was therefore subject to review under the First Amendment. But the majority did not decide whether the law could survive that constitutional analysis. It left that bigger question, once again, to the lower court.

Atypical bedfellows Justices Sotomayor and Alito—arguably the Court's most liberal justice and one of the Court's most conservative, respectively—teamed up to criticize the majority's approach. The Court's decision encouraged piecemeal litigation because the statute's operation was unclear, those justices argued. Given that uncertainty, the Court should have asked New York's top court to decipher what the law actually prohibited before deciding that it regulated speech. Only then could the Supreme Court address whether that regulation passed constitutional muster. The majority's "quarter-loaf outcome is worse than none," Justice Sotomayor wrote for the two justices.

Courting Politics

Narrow opinions like those in *State Farm*, *Salman*, *Bank of America*, and *Expressions Hair Design* are not entirely unique to the Supreme Court's 2016 term. UCLA law professor Richard Re described in 2014 what he called the Roberts Court's "One Last Chance" doctrine, under which the Court avoids resolving a knotty constitutional issue by finding a "barely tenable way" to resolve the issue on narrower grounds. Re's paradigmatic example was the Court's invalidation of part of the Voting Rights Act in *Shelby County v. Holder*. Prior to that decision, the Court had handed down an opinion on a similar case, *Northwest Austin Municipal Utility District No. 1 v. Holder*. There, "the Court adopted an extraordinarily strained statutory reading to avoid what would have been an immediately disruptive result: invalidating the Voting Rights Act's coverage formula. But the Court didn't truly *avoid* the constitutional merits." Instead, "it packed its decision with dicta suggesting that the merits would likely be decided against the Act's constitutionality."

Re notes that one of the benefits of the One Last Chance doctrine is to prepare stakeholders for disruptive Court decisions. After *Northwest Austin*, Congress and the American public were on notice that the VRA's coverage formula was in trouble, thereby affording the political branches a window of time in which to take action. When Congress did not take action to fix the problem, the Court did not hesitate to strike down the coverage formula and defang a large part of the landmark law. But the shock of such a dramatic change to the voting rights landscape was lessened by the Court's earlier signaling.

Such momentous disruptions by the justices, even when expected, risk casting the Supreme Court in a political light, thereby making it susceptible to the kinds of crisis in which it found itself embroiled during the 2016 term. Indeed, the continued striking down of widely supported legislation arguably led to the most well-known crisis in the Court's history: Franklin Delano Roosevelt's infamous court-packing plan. The notorious plan serves as a reminder that a Court seen to be replacing its own views with those of the more politically accountable branches of government is a Court in danger of provoking a strong—and potentially dangerous—reaction from those branches. The tale of the court-packing plan starts in the wake of the Great Depression, when Democrats held both houses of Congress by wide margins. In the 1930s, they passed a series of bills to implement FDR's "New Deal." These laws were aimed at the three *R*s: relief for those most impacted by the 1929 stock market crash; recovery of the financial system; and reform to prevent another similar occurrence. While the president's policies garnered broad support among the public and in Congress, they were met with strong opposition in the Supreme Court. Piece after piece of New Deal legislation was struck down by slim majorities on the high court, with few victories in between.

The last straw for President Roosevelt came in 1936. The case of *Morehead v. New York ex rel. Tipaldo* had come to the Court too late to be decided during its current term. But a conservative bloc of four justices wanted to deal Roosevelt "one more blow" before the upcoming presidential election, according to historian Peter Irons. They therefore hurried the case through the certiorari process and decided the case before the Court went on its summer recess. When the decision came down, the Court split 5–4 over the constitutionality of a minimum wage law out of New York. To support invalidating the law, the five justices in the majority pointed to the Constitution's vague due process clause, prohibiting the government from depriving anyone of "life, liberty or property without due process of law." Reading the provision broadly, the majority said that "the State is without power by any form of legislation to prohibit, change, or nullify contracts between employers and adult women workers."

The *Morehead* decision was met with more criticism from both Democrats and Republicans than any other decision in the New Deal era, according to Irons. Although Roosevelt had been vocal about previous defeats at the Supreme Court, with the presidential election in full swing, Roosevelt did not immediately respond. After winning the 1936 election by a landslide, however, Roosevelt introduced the Judicial Procedures Reform Bill of 1937 in February of that year. Among other things, the bill proposed adding as many as six additional justices to the high court bench, one for every member who was over the age of seventy. The focus on seventy was not an accident, Irons notes, since all four of a bloc of conservative justices that had repeatedly ruled against Roosevelt's New Deal legislation—labeled by the press as the "Four Horsemen"—were elderly.

Though the president cast the bill as a way to ensure that infirm justices did not imperil the judiciary's ability to do its job, the prevailing view was that Roosevelt was attempting to counterweigh his opposition on the high court by appointing justices sure to support his policies. Roosevelt took to his popular fireside chats to counter growing criticism over the bill, and he began to gain some traction. Just a few weeks later in *West Coast Hotel Co. v. Parrish*, the Supreme Court surprised many by upholding a state minimum wage law that was similar to the one it had struck down in *Morehead*. Justice Owen Roberts, who had ruled against economic regulation in *Morehouse*, switched to vote with the liberals to uphold the law at issue in *West Coast Hotel*. The decision was hailed as the end of the notorious *Lochner* era, a time defined by the Court's far-reaching interpretation of the due process clause, which was used to strike down popular legislation a majority of the Court disagreed with. Additionally, Roberts's vote is often referred to as the "switch in time that saved nine" because Roosevelt's court-packing plan would shortly thereafter be defeated in Congress. "FDR's war on the court," as the National Constitution Center puts it, was over.

Although Peter Irons debunks the view that Justice Roberts switched his vote in *West Coast Hotel* in order to fend off Roosevelt's court-packing plan, the constitutional standoff remains a reminder of the fragility of the Supreme Court as an institution. Nevertheless, the Court found itself in the midst of a similar crisis in 2016—namely, the Court was once again pulled into a political battle that threatened to call into question its integrity and independence. Chief Justice Roberts unknowingly weighed in on the issue just ten days before Justice Scalia's passing when he spoke about the political nature of the confirmation process. He seemed to imply that the Senate—not the justices themselves—would be responsible for the Court's future predicament. Although the justices do not work as Republicans or Democrats, that was the "unfortunate perception that the public might get from the confirmation process," he complained. "When you have a sharply political, divisive hearing process, it increases the danger that whoever comes out of it will be viewed in those terms."

But Justice Scalia himself thought just the opposite. The Supreme Court itself was to blame for the partisan nature of the confirmation process, he told the *Today Show* in 2005. Over the past three or four decades, "the Supreme Court has been making more and more political decisions that are not really resolved by the Constitution at all," he said. That cast the Supreme Court in a political light, making the justices' political leanings fair game during the confirmation process.

Many who agree might point to the Supreme Court's *Bush v. Gore* decision, in which the Court embroiled itself in the contentious 2000 presidential contest by halting vote recounts in the pivotal state of Florida. The decision was seen by many, rightly or wrongly, as handing the White House to Republicans by 5–4 partisan vote.

Others point to the blockbuster decision that saved Obamacare from redlining before it even got up and running, *National Federation of Independent Business v.*

Sebelius. There, Chief Justice Roberts shocked conservatives by voting to uphold a vital portion of the law that required Americans to pay a "penalty" if they did not obtain health insurance. The main argument against the penalty was that Congress did not have the power to force Americans to buy health insurance. And although the chief justice agreed with that argument, he found of clever way to avoid striking down the law nonetheless. Instead of viewing the penalty as a punishment for failing to purchase health insurance—something the Court determined Congress could not compel—Chief Justice Roberts interpreted the penalty as a "tax," falling within Congress's broad taxing power. Critics perceived the chief's maneuver as a sleight of hand meant more to avoid an unpopular decision than to faithfully interpret the Constitution.

Justice Scalia himself would likely have pointed to the landmark *Obergefell v. Hodges* decision as an example of the kind of case that cast doubt on the neutrality of the Supreme Court and subjected it to a political hijacking. The case affirmed the right to marry for same-sex couples and invalidated dozens of state constitutional provisions banning the practice. The decision was widely expected given that the vast majority of lower courts had come out that way, with only a few dissenting rulings. But Justice Kennedy's decision for the majority did not do an effective job of explaining why such a result was mandated by the Constitution. Instead, the decision spoke in sweeping terms of "dignity" and "autonomy." The Constitution protects not only the rights enumerated in the Bill of Rights but also "certain personal choices central to individual dignity and autonomy, including intimate choices that define personal identity and beliefs," Justice

Kennedy declared. He concluded with the following declamation:

> No union is more profound than marriage, for it embodies the highest ideals of love, fidelity, devotion, sacrifice, and family. In forming a marital union, two people become something greater than once they were. As some of the petitioners in these cases demonstrate, marriage embodies a love that may endure even past death. It would misunderstand these men and women to say they disrespect the idea of marriage. Their plea is that they do respect it, respect it so deeply that they seek to find its fulfillment for themselves. Their hope is not to be condemned to live in loneliness, excluded from one of civilization's oldest institutions. They ask for equal dignity in the eyes of the law. The Constitution grants them that right.

The language in Justice Kennedy's opinion was beautiful and uplifting. But it sparsely explained the legal reasoning behind the decision. Justice Scalia did not hide his contempt for such soaring language. "If, even as the price to be paid for a fifth vote, I ever joined an opinion for the Court that began: 'The Constitution promises liberty to all within its reach, a liberty that includes certain specific rights that allow persons, within a lawful realm, to define and express their identity,' I would hide my head in a bag," Justice Scalia stingingly wrote. "The Supreme Court of the United States has descended from the disciplined legal reasoning of John Marshall and Joseph Story to the mystical aphorisms of the fortune cookie." The chief put it a bit more gently, though no less significantly: "If you are among the many Americans—of whatever sexual orientation—who favor expanding same-sex marriage, by all means celebrate today's decision. Celebrate the achievement of a desired goal. Celebrate the opportunity for a new expression of commitment to a partner. Celebrate the availability of new benefits. But do not celebrate the Constitution. It had nothing to do with it."

But for many, *Citizens United v. Federal Election Commission* is the prime example of the Court substituting its preferences for that of the peoples' representatives, thereby making the Court susceptible to political chicanery. The landmark campaign finance case came to the Court as a narrow challenge to funding prohibitions that the plaintiffs argued did not apply to them. In particular, a nonprofit group, Citizens United, produced a documentary critical of then senator Hillary Clinton, who was running for president in the 2008 election. Citizens United was worried that if it ran the movie, it might run afoul of the Bipartisan Campaign Reform Act (BCRA) of 2002, which, among many other things, prohibited corporations and unions from spending money to advocate for the election or defeat of a particular candidate. It also prohibited those groups from "publicly distribut[ing]" any "electioneering communications," which are communications that refer to a specific candidate and are made within a certain time frame from the election. It was this last prohibition that Citizens United was worried about violating by distributing its documentary. So the group asked a federal court to make clear that the law did not apply to them. A special district court, made up of three judges, refused to do so.

The case came to the Supreme Court via a special procedure that makes it more likely that the high court will agree to hear the case. And that was exactly what the justices agreed to do in November 2008. After briefing by the parties, the Supreme Court heard argument in the case on March 24, 2009. On the last day of its 2008 term, the Supreme Court still had not decided the case.

On that day, June 29, 2009, the justices shocked court watchers with an order buried on the second page of a four-page list of orders. The "case is restored to the calendar for reargument. The parties are directed to file supplemental brief addressing" a new question of whether the BCRA's prohibitions on corporate and union funding was constitutional. In a 2012 *New Yorker* article, Jeffrey Toobin details the fascinating backstory hidden in that brief order. Chief Justice Roberts had originally written a narrow majority opinion for the Court, saying that Citizens United could not be barred from airing its documentary because it was not an "electioneering communication." Justice Kennedy wrote a broader concurring opinion arguing that the law's limits on corporate and union funding was unconstitutional. That opinion began to win over the other justices in the majority, replacing the chief's more narrow opinion. That drew a scathing dissent by Justice David Souter, who had announced in April that he intended to retire after nearly two decades on the bench. According to Toobin, Souter's dissent was "an extraordinary, bridge-burning farewell to the Court" that "could damage the Court's credibility." In particular, the dissent took issue with the fact that the Supreme Court had decided the case on an issue that was not squarely before it and on which the justices had not been briefed. To solve the problem, the Court reheard the case, this time specifically requiring the parties to address the broader question.

The Court set the reargument for a special session on September 9, 2009, almost a full month before the Supreme Court was scheduled to begin its new term. Two significant Supreme Court happenings occurred between the time the Court first heard the case and the time it held reargument. First, then solicitor general Elena Kagan settled into her role as the government's top attorney at the Supreme Court. Though she had been confirmed as the first woman to hold the post just days before the first *Citizens United* argument, the case was initially argued by career Department of Justice attorney Malcolm Stewart. But by the time September rolled around, Kagan was ready to take up the reins. Incredibly, the September 2009 argument in *Citizens United* was Kagan's first appellate argument. The second significant happening was that Justice Sonia Sotomayor was confirmed to the high court bench. A longtime district court and appellate court judge, Sotomayor was hastened through the confirmation process to fill the vacancy left by Souter. She took her post on August 8, 2009. *Citizens United* was her first Supreme Court argument.

The decision took more than four months for the justices to decide. When they did, they came down along predictable ideological lines. Kennedy, joined by his conservative colleagues, wrote the 5–4 decision striking down the BCRA's prohibitions on corporate and union campaign funding. Kennedy's opinion first explained why the Court could not decide the case on narrower grounds. Such a fact-specific result would create uncertainty in future cases and would therefore chill speech, the Court declared. "The First Amendment does not permit laws that force speakers to retain a campaign finance attorney, conduct demographic marketing research, or seek declaratory rulings before discussing the most salient political issues of our day," the Court said. It would "be remiss" if it accepted such "an unsound principle merely to avoid the necessity of making a broader ruling."

Next, the Court took aim at the bigger prize: the BCRA's prohibitions on corporate and union funding. The Court determined that this was "an outright ban [on speech], backed by criminal sanctions." To explain its conclusion that money was constitutionally protected speech, the Court cited the Supreme Court's 1976 landmark campaign finance decision, *Buckley v. Valeo.* "[As a] restriction on the amount of money a person or group can spend on political communication during a campaign, [that statute] necessarily reduces the quantity of expression by restricting the number of issues discussed, the depth of their exploration, and the size of the audience reached," the Court explained. If applied to individuals, "no one would believe that it is merely a time, place, or manner restriction on speech. Its purpose and effect are to silence entities whose voices the Government deems to be suspect." But speech was "an essential mechanism of democracy, for it is the means to hold officials accountable to the people. . . . The right of citizens to inquire, to hear, to speak, and to use information to reach consensus is a precondition to enlightened self-government and a necessary means to protect it," the Court declared. "For these reasons, political speech must prevail against laws that would suppress it, whether by design or inadvertence."

Finally, the Court rejected the government's anticorruption rationale for supporting such limits on political speech. *Buckley* had held that corruption, or even the appearance of corruption, could justify limits on political speech. But favoritism and influence in politics is not corruption, the Court said. Only "quid pro quo corruption"— "dollars for political favors," as the Supreme Court said both before and after *Citizens United*—would provide a sufficient rationale for curbing First Amendment rights.

The job of calling out the majority this time fell to Justice John Paul Stevens, one of the longest serving justices in the Court's history. As the most senior justice in the minority, Justice Stevens had originally assigned the case to Souter, according to Toobin's account. With Souter gone, Stevens took up the role. He spent around twenty minutes reading from his dissent in *Citizens United* from the bench—an occurrence limited to the weightiest disagreements between the justices. "The language in his written dissent was forceful," *CBS News*'s Jan Crawford noted. Stevens called the majority's result "profoundly misguided" and took it to task for "manufacturing" the case to get the result it wanted. "Essentially, five justices were unhappy with the limited nature of the case before us, so they changed the case to give themselves an opportunity to change the law," Stevens wrote. "The novelty of the Court's procedural dereliction . . . [was] matched by the novelty of its ruling on the merits. . . . In a democratic society, the longstanding consensus on the need to limit corporate campaign spending should outweigh the wooden application of judge-made rules." The majority had elevated corporations to a level not seen since the Court's notorious *Lochner* era, Stevens suggested. "At bottom, the Court's opinion is thus a rejection of the common sense of the American people, who have recognized a need to prevent corporations from undermining self-government since the founding, and who have fought against the distinctive corrupting potential of corporate electioneering since the days of Theodore Roosevelt. It is a strange time to repudiate that common sense. While American democracy is imperfect, few outside the majority of this Court would have thought its flaws included a dearth of corporate money in politics. . . . I emphatically dissent," Justice Stevens concluded.

Despite the historical warning of the court-packing plan and the Court's recent experience during its 2016 term, the justices do not seem inclined to chart a more moderate course. Indeed, the Court is primed to continue what has been called by critics as the "Lochnerization of the First Amendment"—the push to use the First Amendment as a weapon to strike down democratically enacted statutes. The name is based on the Supreme Court's infamous 1905 case *Lochner v. New York*, in which it struck down state limits on working hours for bakers. This was where the Court developed its broad interpretation of the due process clause as protecting an inviolable right for parties to contract with one another. New York could not interfere with the right of employers to negotiate directly with their employees over working conditions, the Supreme Court said in *Lochner*. The case ushered in an era in which the Supreme Court aggressively struck down regulations aimed at protecting workers, and the *Lochner* era is notorious in the legal world as a time when the Court substituted its policy preferences for those of elected—and more accountable—officials.

One case, *Janus v. State, County, and Municipal Employees, Council 31*, which the justices have been asked to review in their 2017 term, will test whether the Supreme Court intends to continue down this path or will change course as a result of its recent experience. *Janus* is the latest in a string of cases that threatens union funding schemes in about two dozen states. In *Janus*, the justices are asked to reconsider a forty-year-old case upholding state laws that allow unions to charge nonmembers "agency fees" to pay for the cost of collective bargaining. Unionized teachers supporting the fees say nonmembers should not be allowed to benefit from the union's protective employment terms while refusing to pay for the union's services. Nonmembers, however, say that in addition to paying for parts of collective bargaining that they agree with—like, perhaps, increased benefits—they are also forced to pay for policies for which they vehemently disagree, like teacher tenure. That runs afoul of the First Amendment, they argue. And the Supreme Court's more conservative justices appear to agree.

The Court has twice come close to overturning *Abood v. Detroit Bd. of Education*, its previous ruling upholding these laws. On the last day of the Supreme Court's 2013 term, Justice Alito stopped just short of doing so in *Harris v. Quinn*. The Court's reasoning in Abood "is questionable on several grounds," Alito said. But he did not expressly overrule it, choosing instead to confine *Abood* to its particular facts and decide *Harris* on different grounds. But the very next term, *Abood* seemed destined to be struck down. In June 2015, the Court agreed to hear *Friedrichs v. California Teachers Association*, in which a group of teachers specifically asked the Supreme Court to strike down its decades-old *Abood* decision. There was not another ground on which the Court could decide this case. Oral argument in January 2016 confirmed that the five conservative justices were ready to overturn the law. But before the Court handed down its decision in that case, Justice Scalia passed away. A little more than a month later, the Court announced its decision on *Friedrichs*: the justices were evenly divided, and *Abood* stood for another day.

The Priceless Value of Citizenship

As the final arbiter of the law, the Supreme Court cannot wholly avoid politically charged controversies. A case in point is President Trump's divisive travel ban.

On January 27, 2017, President Trump issued an executive order, "Protecting the Nation from Foreign Terrorist Entry into the United States." Citing the devastating terror attacks of September 11, 2001, and the numerous foreign-born individuals who "have been convicted or implicated in terrorism-related crimes since," the president ordered a temporary pause of entry into the country by individuals from seven predominantly Muslim countries. The Obama administration had already designated these countries as presenting a heightened risk of terrorism. The Trump administration's pause on travel from these countries would allow it to evaluate current visa screening measures for these countries "to ensure that adequate standards are established to prevent infiltration by foreign terrorists or criminals." Causing chaos at airports, the order was immediately challenged across the country.

Those challenging what would become known as the travel ban pointed to then candidate Trump's anti-Muslim statements during the 2016 presidential campaign. Early in the race, the Trump campaign noted its intention to implement "a total and complete shutdown of Muslims entering the United States until our country's representatives can figure out what is going on." Trump asserted (via Twitter) that the policy was necessary to curb "the extraordinary influx of hatred & danger coming into our country." Months later, following allegations that such a religious-based ban would run afoul of the Constitution, the Trump campaign switched to a regionally focused ban. In the first weeks of rolling out this new policy, Trump told NBC's *Meet the Press* that the focus was now on territories because people "were so upset when I used the word Muslim. Oh, you can't use the word Muslim. . . . And I'm okay with that, because I'm talking territory instead of Muslim." Now president Trump's executive order was nothing but a sham, challengers claimed. And the president did not do himself any favors when he said at the signing of the executive order that "this is the 'Protection of the Nation from Foreign Terrorist Entry into the United States.' We all know what that means."

By week's end, the president's executive order had been stayed nationwide by a federal district court in Washington. The plaintiffs were likely to prevail on their claims that the executive order violated the Constitution or the Immigration and Nationality Act, the district court said. After the nationwide stay was affirmed by the Ninth Circuit, the Trump administration tweaked the ban to address some of the courts' concerns. The second executive order dropped one country completely from the ban but left in place many of the other controversial issues related to the other six countries. The new executive order, though, did attempt to strengthen the justifications for continuing to include those countries. Iran, Libya, Somalia, Sudan, Syria, and Yemen "warrant additional scrutiny in connection with our immigration policies because the conditions in these countries present heightened threats," the new executive order explained. "Each of these countries is a state sponsor of terrorism, has been significantly compromised by terrorist organizations, or contains active conflict zones. Any of these circumstances diminishes the foreign government's willingness or ability to share or validate important information about individuals seeking to travel to the United States. Moreover, the significant presence in each of these countries of terrorist organizations, their members, and others exposed to those organizations increases the chance that conditions will be exploited to enable terrorist operatives or sympathizers to travel to the United States."

The changes, though, did not allay the concerns of those suing to stop the travel ban. They renewed their lawsuits, challenging the revised ban both constitutionally and statutorily. After months of fast-tracked briefing and oral argument, the Fourth Circuit, which was considering a parallel challenge to the travel ban, divided along partisan lines to halt the travel ban until the federal courts had more time to review the merits of the challengers' claims. Those challengers included US citizens and lawful permanent residents who sought entry for one of their family members from one of the restricted countries. Although the executive order was written in a facially neutral manner, President Trump's comments, both before and after the election, demonstrated that the true purpose behind the act was religious, the Fourth Circuit said. Previous case law had precluded looking beyond the "four corners" of the challenged law to statements made by the law's backers, except when, as here, there was bad faith in adopting the law. "Just as the reasonable observer's 'world is not made brand new every morning,'" the court said, "nor are we able to awake without the vivid memory of these statements. We cannot shut our eyes to such evidence when it stares us in the face, for 'there's none so blind as they that won't see.'" Because the travel ban was intended to disfavor Muslims more than other those of religions, it likely could not stand constitutional scrutiny, the Fourth Circuit concluded.

The decision sparked several dissents from Republican-appointed judges. They accused the majority of fabricating a new rule of law in order to second-guess the president, something that was extremely inappropriate in light of the complex national security matters at issue, in which the judiciary had no expertise. Moreover, critics of the Fourth Circuit's decision emphasized a point conceded by the challengers at oral argument: given that the executive order was neutral on its face, it very well may have been constitutional under any other president without the same ostensible bias against Muslims. The attack on the travel ban, the critics said, was merely another attack on the unpopular president.

At the same time the Fourth Circuit was considering the travel ban, the Ninth Circuit was considering its case too. However, with less than a month before the Supreme

Court's 2016 term was set to expire, the administration decided not to wait until the Ninth Circuit weighed in to ask the Supreme Court to step in. Before the Ninth Circuit could hand down its opinion, the government asked the justices to stay the lower courts' rulings, effectively reinstating the ban nationwide. The hurry, the government said, was because national security was at issue. With each passing day that the administration was required to admit individuals from these countries, the more likely it was that a terrorist would slip through the borders, the government argued.

On June 12, the day that the challengers of the travel ban were scheduled to file their briefs in the case, the Ninth Circuit handed down its opinion, throwing yet another wrinkle into the case. Instead of deciding the case on constitutional grounds like the Fourth Circuit, the Ninth Circuit found that President Trump had overstepped his statutory authority. The Immigration and Nationality Act "gives the President broad powers to control the entry of aliens," the Ninth Circuit conceded. "But immigration, even for the President, is not a one-person show." Before invoking those broad powers, the president must meet certain preconditions. In particular, the administration pointed to a provision in the act that states, "Whenever the President finds that the entry of any aliens or of any class of aliens into the United States would be detrimental to the interests of the United States, he may by proclamation, and for such period as he shall deem necessary, suspend the entry of all aliens or any class of aliens as immigrants or nonimmigrants, or impose on the entry of aliens any restrictions he may deem to be appropriate." That provision required that before the president could suspend travel for more than 180 million nationals from the six prohibited countries, he was required to specifically find that the entry of those aliens would be detrimental to the United States. The president had not done so here, the court determined. For example, although the executive order noted certain conditions in the specified nations that could make its nationals more susceptible to terrorist activities, the government had not shown why the current screening protocols were insufficient to screen such individuals out. The court pointed to a Department of Homeland Security report that was leaked shortly after the first executive order. Nationality was not a reliable indicator of future terrorist activity, the report said. Moreover, citizens of the prohibited countries were rarely implicated in US-based terrorism. Among the terrorist attacks since 2001, slightly "more than half were U.S. citizens born in the United States," the court said. Of the six countries still precluded under the ban, "only Somalia was identified as being among the 'top' countries-of-origin for the terrorists analyzed in the report," with three such offenders.

For more than two weeks, the country waited for word from the US Supreme Court. As time passed, it became more and more likely that the Supreme Court would not say anything on the fate of the travel ban until the last day of the term, scheduled for June 26, 2017—the last Monday in June. On "opinion Mondays," the Court typically hands down an order list at nine thirty a.m. before handing down opinions at ten. Included in the order list is whether the Supreme Court has agreed to hear a given case and other orders related to cases that the Supreme Court has not yet agreed to take up. The ten o'clock opinion time is usually reserved for the issuance of opinions in cases that the Supreme Court has fully briefed and argued.

Court watchers eagerly awaited the order list on the morning of June 26. Besides a notable grant dealing with religious exemptions from antidiscrimination laws, the order list was otherwise unremarkable. There was no mention of the government's request to reinstate the travel ban while it worked its way through the federal courts and no word if the Supreme Court would hear the case itself. The next opportunity would likely be the following day, when the Court issued its end-of-the-term "clean-up" list. First, though, the Supreme Court had to hand down its remaining cases of the term. At ten o'clock, it issued opinions in four of the remaining six cases. The other two cases, the chief announced, would be reargued the next term because the justices were evenly split. But that was not the end of the Court's business. The chief's final announcement was that the Supreme Court was partially reinstating the travel ban and would set oral argument for October 2017, when it returned from summer recess.

The Trump administration immediately claimed victory. "Today's unanimous Supreme Court decision is a clear victory for our national security. It allows the travel suspension for the six terror-prone countries and the refugee suspension to become largely effective," a statement from the president said. The use of the term "unanimous" was intriguing given that three justices had specifically dissented from the Court's unsigned opinion to partially revive the travel ban. But the wording was likely due to the fact that the three noted dissents—including Trump's appointee to the bench, Justice Gorsuch—would have reinstated the ban in full, without conditions. But more reflection on the wording of the Supreme Court's decision cut back on the president's victory. Notably, the Supreme Court refused to allow the travel ban to go into effect against the specific plaintiffs in this case. More significantly, the Court had also prohibited the Trump administration from enforcing the ban against anyone with a "credible claim of a bona fide relationship with a person or entity in the United States." Such a bona fide relationship would include the spouse of a lawful permanent resident or a foreign student already admitted to a US university. But the Court did not set out clear rules as to whom the ban could lawfully be applied to.

That vague language was likely purposeful, masking sharp disagreement among the justices as to the legality of the underlying executive order. Indeed, former solicitor general Gregory Garre said the ambiguous language seemed crafted to keep as many justices as possible from dissenting from the Supreme Court's order. But Justice Thomas, joined by Justices Alito and Gorsuch, could not sign onto the order in full. The Court's imprecise remedy would "prove unworkable," Thomas said. The "compromise will burden executive officials with the task of deciding—on peril of contempt—whether individuals from the six affected nations who wish to enter the United States have a sufficient connection to a person or entity in this country." It will also "invite a flood of litigation until this case is finally resolved on the merits." The Court should have lifted the ban in full to avoid such confusion, Thomas argued.

He proved correct. The Trump administration announced that the ban would go into partial effect on June 29. But as of June 28, the administration had not defined what counted as a "bona fide relationship." Not until the morning that the ban was set to go into effect did the administration clarify that it would interpret "bona fide relationship" to include "a parent (including parent-in-law), spouse, child, adult son or daughter, fiancé(e), son-in-law, daughter-in-law, and sibling, whether whole or half," including step relations, according to the Department of Homeland Security. Such a relationship did not include "grandparents, grandchildren, aunts, uncles, nieces, nephews, cousins, brothers-in-law and sisters-in-law and any other 'extended' family members." And when the narrowed travel ban finally went into effect—after a several-hour delay—new lawsuits popped up challenging the administration's interpretation of the Supreme Court's order. Eventually the Supreme Court would weigh in to clarify the reach of its previous order. In doing so, the Court once again handed down a quasi win for both the plaintiffs and the government.

This reach for consensus by tending toward an equivocal result was not the only indication that the high court was quite divided when it came to the issue of immigration. The Court's inability to come to a majority result in the highly charged challenge to President Obama's deferred action immigration program during the 2015 term was perhaps one of the strongest examples of the Court's inability to operate while shorthanded.

In 2012, the Obama administration announced that certain young adults who entered the country illegally when they were children would be allowed a temporary reprieve from the threat of deportation. They would also be given work authorization, allowing them to work while on deferral. To be eligible for the program, these so-called dreamers would have to meet several prerequisites, including longtime residence in the United States and lack of a criminal record. More than 600,000 applications were approved under the DACA—or Deferred Action of Childhood Arrivals—program from 2012 to 2014, according to a federal court that would later review the legality of the president's program.

Many criticized DACA as an amnesty program that would only encourage others to cross the border illegally. Others, however, said dreamers brought to the country as kids had not done anything wrong and were now contributing members of US society. The administration emphasized the fact that Congress had not appropriated enough funds to deport all illegal immigrants from the United States. Therefore, while the administration focused on deporting serious criminals, DACA recipients should be allowed to work and contribute to the economy. Despite this ongoing debate, the Obama administration expanded DACA in 2014. The administration adopted the Deferred Action for Parents of Americans and Lawful Permanent Residents, or DAPA, program. The program once again deferred deportation and granted work authorization, this time to parents of US citizens or lawful permanent residents. DAPA dramatically expanded the number of individuals eligible for deferred immigration action. "Of the approximately 11.3 million illegal aliens in the United States, 4.3 million would be eligible for lawful presence pursuant to DAPA," a federal court explained.

As had become popular during the Obama administration, Texas led a coalition of Republican-dominated states in a legal challenge to the expanded DACA program and the DAPA program in whole. It argued that the programs were adopted in violation of the Administrative Procedure Act (APA), a federal law that dictates how government agencies can enact binding regulations. Moreover, even if the administration had complied with the APA, the policy would still be voidable because it contravened Congress's comprehensive statutes regarding when aliens were permitted to work in the country, Texas argued. The administration responded that it had broad discretion in prioritizing the deportation of immigrants, especially in light of the fact that it was impossible to deport all immigrants unlawfully present in the United States.

A district judge sitting in Texas—who seemed specifically shopped by the states to rule against the administration—barred the government from carrying out its DAPA program until the court could consider whether the president had in fact overstepped his bounds. After the Fifth Circuit affirmed, the Obama administration hurried to get the case to the Supreme Court in time for it to be heard during the 2015 term. If the Supreme Court did not acquiesce to its request to hurry along briefing in the case, the government threatened to seek a special session of the high court to specifically consider the government's plea. The justices avoided the special session by expeditiously considering the parties' briefs, and on January 19, 2016, the Supreme Court agreed to hear the case. Once again, Justice Scalia's death changed the legal landscape dramatically. On June 23, 2016, the Supreme Court announced its decision in *United States v. Texas*. "The judgment is affirmed by an equally divided Court," the Court's unsigned opinion said in full.

That same division in immigration cases persisted during the Court's 2016 term. On the last day of its 2016 term, the Supreme Court once against delivered an unexpected decision. Two cases dealing with so-called crimimmigration issues—immigration cases that often have criminal implications or vice versa—were "restored to the calendar for reargument." At issue in one, *Jennings v. Rodriguez*, was whether immigrants awaiting deportation proceeding are entitled to a bond hearing. Immigration and Customs Enforcement "detains more than 429,000 individuals over the course of a year, with roughly 33,000 individuals in detention on any given day," according to the Ninth Circuit, which considered the question before the Supreme Court did. Many of those individuals would have legitimate defenses to deportation, allowing them to stay in the United States. But those individuals spent, on average, 404 days in immigration detention before they could press those claims with an immigration judge and prevail. Given the draconian effects of that delay for those that would ultimately prevail in their immigration cases, all circuits that were asked to decide the question agreed that bond hearings were required. The only difference in their decisions was when those bond hearings would be due.

Having lost on this issue in six different circuit courts of appeal, the federal government brought its case to the Supreme Court. The Court's agreement to hear the case was not a good sign for those in favor of bond hearings. The Supreme Court reverses the lower courts in most cases that it agrees to hear. During its 2016 term, the Court reversed or vacated the lower court's judgment in approximately three-quarters of the cases it decided. Moreover, the chances for reversal in *Jennings* were increased due to the fact that the circuit courts had all agreed that bond hearings were required. There was no reason for the Supreme Court to step in if those courts got it right.

During oral argument in November, though, the justices seemed evenly split on the question presented. Some justices seemed to want to say that bond hearings were required under the Constitution. Others were concerned the Court could not do that because the Ninth Circuit had confined itself to a more narrow ruling. Bond hearings were required under the immigration statutes, the Ninth Circuit said, avoiding the constitutional issue. Two weeks after the case was argued before the justices, they ordered the parties to submit "supplemental briefing." The parties were "directed" to squarely address the constitutional issue. It seemed that the justices might hand immigrants an even bigger victory than they had won below.

But month after month, the Supreme Court's decision in the *Jennings* case was not released. During its 2016 term, the Court took just under 100 days on average to hand down an opinion after it had been argued. The shortest time from argument to opinion was by Chief Justice Roberts, at 35 days; the longest, a crimmigration case by Justice Ginsburg, took 216. By the last day of the term, the *Jennings* case had been outstanding for 209 days. But there was more waiting ahead. Presumably split 4–4 over the question, the Supreme Court set the case for reargument next term, when there would be a ninth justice to break the tie.

The same fate befell *Sessions v. Dimaya*, yet another crimmigration case. *Dimaya* asked whether a provision in the Immigration and Nationality Act requiring removal for certain serious criminal offenses was unconstitutionally vague because it did not put immigrants on fair notice of what conduct subjected them to deportation. In 2015, the Supreme Court struck down similar language in the Armed Career Criminal Act as too vague to withstand constitutional scrutiny. That case, *Johnson v. United States,* was overshadowed that term by blockbusters in same-sex marriage, Obamacare, and the death penalty, but *Johnson* had implications that continue to reverberate through the justice system. Indeed, the Supreme Court itself heard another *Johnson* case during its 2016 term, in which it determined that *Johnson's* vagueness determination did not apply to the quasi-mandatory Federal Sentencing Guidelines. Although the justices were able to come to a 5–2 decision in that sentencing case, they were dead-locked 4–4 over whether *Johnson's* vagueness analysis was applicable in the realm of immigration law. Along with *Jennings,* the justices had to reconsider the case during its 2017 term, when Justice Gorsuch would be available to break the tie.

But while immigration cases have often stumped the justices over the last few terms, there has also been some broad consensus in this area. Such was the case in *Sessions v. Morales-Santana.* In that case, twenty days would end up making all the difference in the world to Luis Ramon Morales-Santana. Morales-Santana's father was that number of days short of meeting an important deadline when he moved from the United States to the Dominican Republic. Presumably unbeknownst to the father, his US citizenship could only be conferred on his later-born son if he had stayed in the United States five years past his fourteenth birthday. Morales-Santana's father left the country just twenty days before his nineteenth birthday. Almost eighty years later, that decision would prove to be critical for his son.

In 2000, the federal government sought to deport Morales-Santana based on several convictions he had received in New York. Morales-Santana claimed the government could not deport him to his home country because his home country was the United States. In particular, while Morales-Santana acknowledged that his father had not technically fulfilled the statutory time requirements to confer citizenship on him, he argued he was nevertheless entitled to citizenship because of the country's disparate treatment of men and women. Under US law, a male unmarried US citizen—like Morales-Santana's father—could only bestow citizenship on his foreign-born child if he had been present in the United States for at least ten years, five of which took place after the father's fourteenth birthday. The law, the government argued, was meant to ensure that there was a sufficient connection between the father and the United States to justify awarding the awesome privilege of citizenship on his foreign-born child.

Importantly, however, the United States significantly relaxed this residency requirement for unwed US citizen mothers. These mothers could pass on their US citizenship so long as they resided one year in the United States. A shortened residency requirement was necessary to reduce statelessness among the children of US citizens, the government argued. When Congress passed the law at issue in *Morales-Santana* in 1940, many countries recognized the mother as the sole parent of a child born out of wedlock. Further, many countries doled out citizenship only if the father was a citizen of that country. As a result, "when a U.S.-citizen mother had a child out of wedlock abroad . . . her child was at great risk of being born stateless unless

U.S. law provided U.S. citizenship for the child," the government explained.

The Supreme Court unanimously rejected this justification for treating the sexes differently. The citizenship laws relating to foreign-born children "date from an era when the lawbooks of our Nation were rife with overbroad generalizations about the way men and women are," Justice Ginsburg wrote for the unanimous Court.

Long before the Court handed down its final decision in *Morales-Santana*, the writing on the wall seemed to be that the Court would hold such distinctions based on sex intolerable under the Constitution's Equal Protection Clause. That was because by May, it seemed extremely likely that Justice Ginsburg would be writing the decision in *Morales-Santana*. The Court, to the best extent possible, tries to ensure that the workload of the justices is evenly distributed, both across the term and throughout the argument sittings. Every other justice had written an opinion for the sitting in which *Morales-Santana* was argued except Justice Ginsburg. In fact, Justice Breyer had already written two cases from that sitting. That meant Justice Ginsburg would likely write *Morales-Santana*.

Given that likelihood, Justice Ginsburg's trailblazing record on women's rights seemed to indicate that the Court would not permit such gender distinctions. Ginsburg had cofounded the Women's Rights Project at the American Civil Liberties Union in the 1970s. She had eventually become the group's general counsel. In her time at the ACLU, she had argued six cases at the Supreme Court, winning an impressive five. In those cases, she had attacked the stereotypical roles of men and women, even if they tended to benefit the female sex at the detriment of men. For example, in *Weinberger v. Wiesenfeld*, Ginsburg argued that the Social Security Act ran afoul of the Constitution's protection of equal rights because it gave more benefits to the wife of a deceased husband than it did to the husband of a deceased wife. The supposition that "male workers' earnings are vital to the support of their families, while the earnings of female wage earners do not significantly contribute to their families' support" was an "archaic and overbroad" generalization that could not be tolerated under the Constitution, the Supreme Court said in *Weinberger*.

Justice Ginsburg cited her victory in *Weinberger* in striking down the unequitable statute in *Morales-Santana*. Today, laws that treat men and women differently based on antiquated notions of proper gender roles were disfavored under the Constitution, Ginsburg said, and so such laws would be treated with heightened skepticism. The justifications unpinning the statutes at issue in *Morales-Santana* were just such an example of the "once habitual, but now untenable, assumptions" pervading our country's laws—namely, that in marriage, the "husband is dominant, wife subordinate." Such "overbroad generalizations" could not justify gender distinctions abhorrent to the Constitution, she concluded.

But the remedy Justice Ginsburg crafted for *Morales-Santana* garnered distain from the progressive community. The Supreme Court, as a nonlegislative body, did not have the power to alter the clear discriminatory wording of the statute, Ginsburg explained. That was a job for Congress alone. Until Congress had the chance to sort it out, the default rule would be that all parents would have to meet the more demanding citizenship-conferral requirements applicable to unwed US citizen fathers. The Court often "levels down" when striking down a discriminatory statute—that is, the Court will extend the favorable treatment to all groups rather than require them all to meet the more stringent requirements. It was clear, though, that if Congress had to choose between requiring both men and women to meet the harsher residency requirements or relaxing them for both, it would have chosen the former, Ginsburg said. As support, she noted that the stricter rule was applicable to both married mothers and fathers. "Put to the choice, Congress, we believe, would have abrogated" the statutes exception for unwed US citizen mothers, "preferring preservation of the general rule," Ginsburg wrote for the Court.

The Court reached similar consensus in *Maslenjak v. United States*—a fair contender for the Court's so-called outrage docket. Every couple of terms, a case comes along that, quite simply, seems to irk the justices. Often the case involves the federal government broadly reading criminal statutes to prosecute an individual for something that seems—to the common observer, at least—to be outside of the law's scope. One case in particular springs to mind. In *Bond v. United States*, the federal government used a chemical weapons treaty to prosecute a scorned lover. In 2006, Carol Anne Bond learned that her closest friend was pregnant. (Good news.) With Bond's husband's baby. (Bad news.) Carol Anne, a microbiologist, sought revenge. She stole chemicals from her office, intending to give her former friend a rash. Bond spread those chemicals on her husband's paramour's car door and mailbox. When the federal authorities found out about her activities, they "naturally charged Bond with two counts of mail theft," Chief Justice Roberts wrote for the Court in 2014.

"More surprisingly," however, federal prosecutors also charged Bond "with two counts of possessing and using a chemical weapon," Roberts wrote. Those charges were brought under statutes implementing the international Convention on Chemical Weapons. The need for such a convention was exemplified by John Singer Sargent's 1919 painting *Gassed*, Roberts said. "The nearly life-sized work depicts two lines of soldiers, blinded by mustard gas, clinging single file to orderlies guiding them to an improvised aid station. There they would receive little treatment and no relief; many suffered for weeks only to have the gas claim their lives. The soldiers were shown staggering through piles of comrades too seriously burned to even join the procession." What Bond did, "an amateur attempt by a jilted wife to injure her husband's lover, which ended up causing only a minor thumb burn readily treated by rinsing with water," bore little resemblance to World War I's Second Battle of Arras depicted by Sargent.

The Supreme Court unanimously scoffed at such a broad application of the chemical weapons statutes. Those laws, intending to curb international threats, did not apply to the kind of "purely local" crimes at issue in *Bond*. Sure, the statute could be read to reach that broadly. But the "notion that some things 'go without saying' applies to legislation just as it does to everyday life," the Court said.

The government's position in *Maslenjak* seemed to similarly annoy the justices. The government had stripped Divna Maslenjak of her US citizenship because she had lied on her citizenship application. The lie certainly seemed consequential. She had said her husband was in danger in their home country of Bosnia because he had avoided military service in the Bosnian Serb Army during the country's years-long civil war. In fact, not only had her husband served in the Bosnia Serb Army, he had served in a brigade that was involved in the infamous slaughter of approximately eight thousand Bosnian Muslims. But the government contended that the significance of her lie did not matter. Maslenjak could be stripped of her US citizenship for any lie, no matter how small, on her citizenship application.

The government's position would prove troublesome for its lawyer during oral argument. Arguing on behalf of the government, Robert Parker began simply enough: "Naturalization is the highest privilege the United States can bestow upon an individual," Parker said. "Congress has required that individuals who seek that high privilege must scrupulously comply with every rule governing the naturalization process." And that was when the chief jumped in. "But, scrupulously," the chief interjected. "I've looked at the naturalization form, there is a question. It's number 22. 'Have you ever,' and they've got 'ever' in bold point, 'committed, assisted in committing, or attempted to commit a crime or offense for which you were not arrested?'" The chief then humorously informed the courtroom that sometime "outside the statute of limitations"— that is, outside of the time period in which a person can be sued for wrongdoing—he had driven over the speed limit at some point in his life. "Now, you say that if I answer that question 'no,' 20 years after I was naturalized as a citizen, you can knock on my door and say, 'Guess what, you're not an American citizen after all.'"

It got worse for Parker from there. The citizenship application asked for every name the applicant had ever gone by, Justice Sotomayor noted. Did that mean that if she did not disclose an embarrassing nickname bullies called her in elementary school that she could be denaturalized? Justice Kagan joined the fun too. Given that the naturalization form asked for your weight, she said she was "horrified" to know that lying about her weight could have those kinds of consequences.

The worst, however, came from Justice Kennedy. Parker attempted to allay the justices' fears by noting that the denaturalized citizen could sometime in the future seek legal status in the United States again. Parker's argument demeaned "the priceless value of citizenship," Kennedy said. Even if Maslenjak could later be restored to her status, that was "not what citizenship means. . . . You're arguing for the government of the United States, talking about what citizenship is and ought to mean."

Not surprisingly, the Supreme Court was unanimous in its rejection of the government's position. The government could not strip citizenship based on an immaterial lie, the Court said. The government had to show that the lie "played some role" in acquiring citizenship.

Macabre Challenges

The Supreme Court's inability to stay out of the frequently controversial issue of immigration was matched by the Court's failure—or refusal—to avoid socially divisive criminal matters. Indeed, the Court took significant steps on criminal subjects that have caused social upheaval in recent years, including racial bias in the criminal justice system, the ability to hold state and federal officers accountable for constitutional violations, and the death penalty mechanism.

One of the Court's most dramatic cases in the 2016 term, *Buck v. Davis*, centered on one of these contentious topics. In July 1995, Duane Buck murdered his ex-girlfriend, Debra Gardner, and her friend. On hearing shots, "Gardner fled the house, and Buck followed," Chief Justice Roberts detailed in his opinion for the Court. Gardner's young children followed too. "While Gardner's son and daughter begged for their mother's life, Buck shot Gardner in the chest." She later died from her wounds.

A jury in Texas sentenced Buck to death. But before doing so, it heard the testimony of Dr. Walter Quijano. A key issue at Buck's sentencing was whether he would be a danger to the prison population if sentenced only to life imprisonment rather than to death. Dr. Quijano, testifying on the defendant's behalf, ultimately concluded that Buck would not be a danger if allowed to live since his crime was one of jealousy, not a more callous emotion. But one thing did make Buck more likely to pose a risk to the prison population, according to Dr. Quijano: Buck's race. "It's a sad commentary that minorities, Hispanics and black people, are over represented in the Criminal Justice System," Dr. Quijano said. Therefore, because Buck was black, he was more likely to commit a violent crime while in prison.

Dr. Quijano's testimony was so egregious that it had actually already reached the Supreme Court in another case where he had similarly handicapped a defendant because of his race. In that case, the Texas attorney general "confessed error," agreeing that the insertion of race into the sentencing was unacceptable and that the case should be retried. The Supreme Court agreed and summarily vacated the sentence and remanded for another sentencing.

That led the Texas Attorney General's Office to conduct an audit of similar cases that might be tainted by Dr. Quijano's racial testimony. The state identified six cases, including Buck's. "By the close of 2002, the Attorney General had confessed error, waived any available procedural defenses, and consented to resentencing in the cases of five of those six defendants," the chief explained. "Not, however, in Buck's." In the other five cases, the state itself had introduced Dr. Quijano's testimony. But in Buck's case, it was his own defense attorney who had introduced the offensive testimony. The defendant should not be given the windfall of a new sentencing based on the mistakes of his own defense counsel, the state argued. By a vote of 6–2, the Supreme Court disagreed. "In fact, the distinction could well cut the other way," the Court said. A jury understood that a prosecutor's role was to convict the defendant, so its members were likely to take evidence submitted by the prosecutor with a grain of salt. When it was the defendant's own lawyer, though, the evidence was "more likely to be taken at face value," the Court explained.

Such consideration of race was "odious in all aspects" but "especially pernicious in the administration of justice," the Court declared. In finding for Buck, the Court rejected the lower courts' determination that the consideration of race was so insignificant in the face of all the other evidence against Buck that it essentially did not matter. "As an initial matter, this is a disturbing departure from a basic premise of our criminal justice system: Our law punishes people for what they do, not who they are," the Court said. Moreover, any consideration of race—however slight—in the criminal justice system "poisons public confidence in the judicial process. . . . Some toxins can be deadly in small doses."

A similar concern for the trustworthiness of the criminal justice system underlined the Court's decision in *Peña-Rodriguez v. Colorado*. Here, instead of infiltrating the sentencing decision, race was interjected into the jury room. Miguel Angel Peña-Rodriguez was charged and convicted of a form of sexual assault on a child after two teenage sisters were accosted in a public bathroom. Following the verdict, two jurors came to Peña-Rodriguez's lawyers to express concern about one juror. The wearisome juror had indicated bias against Peña-Rodriguez because of his Mexican heritage. "I think he did it because he's Mexican and Mexican men take whatever they want," the juror was said to have proclaimed. In the juror's experience, "nine times out of ten Mexican men were guilty of being aggressive toward women and young girls."

The facts call to mind *Buck*'s admonition that such obvious racial bias is "odious" to the criminal justice system. But Peña-Rodriguez's attorneys ran into a centuries-old rule touching on the sanctity of jury deliberations. The Supreme Court itself cited a 1785 decision relying on the so-called no-impeachment rule, which precludes juror testimony on jury deliberations with the goal of overturning the jury's verdict. The concern is that such testimony could chill the frank deliberations required in the jury room. As such, every state and the federal system has a version of the rule, and the Supreme Court itself has been particularly protective of this concept. Just a couple of terms ago, the Court refused to allow evidence that suggested one juror had lied to the trial court about her inability to be impartial. More astonishing, in 1987, the Court even precluded evidence that jurors had been under the influence of drugs and alcohol during jury deliberations.

The Court, however, thought race was a special case. "All forms of improper bias pose challenges to the trial process," Justice Kennedy wrote for the 5–3 Court. "But there is a sound basis to treat racial bias with added precaution. A constitutional rule that racial bias in the justice system must be addressed—including, in some instances, after the verdict has been entered—is necessary to prevent a systemic loss of confidence in jury verdicts, a confidence that is a central premise of the Sixth Amendment trial right," he said. Writing in the sweeping style common to Justice Kennedy's opinions, he concluded that the "[n]ation must continue to make strides to overcome race-based discrimination." The Court's decision sought "to strengthen the broader principle that society can and must move forward by achieving the thoughtful, rational dialogue at the foundation of both the jury system and the free society that sustains our Constitution."

Finally, while not as explicit as in *Buck* and *Peña-Rodriguez*, race seemed to be lurking in the background of the Supreme Court's revival of Elijah Manuel's suit against the Illinois police. According to Manuel, his brother was pulled over in the early morning hours of March 18, 2011, for failing to signal before a turn. Manuel, riding in the passenger seat, was dragged from the car by one of the officers, who "called him a racial slur, and kicked and punched him as he lay on the ground," the Court explained. After searching Manuel, the cops found a vitamin bottle with pills in it, which they tested for illegal drugs. "The test came back negative for any controlled substance, leaving the officers with no evidence that Manuel had committed a crime. . . . Still, the officers arrested Manuel and took him to the" police station. Back at the station, Manuel fared no better. Although another test came back negative for illicit drugs, the technician lied, claiming that one of the pills tested positive for ecstasy. Manuel was charged with possession of a controlled substance. Subsequently, a judge reviewed Manuel's charge and, based on the fabricated evidence, sent Manuel to jail to await trial. A third test was eventually done on the pills, revealing that the pills were not illegal. Manuel was not released from jail, however, until about a month later. "In all, he had spent 48 days in pretrial detention," the Supreme Court explained.

Manuel sued the Illinois town and the police officers for violating his Fourth Amendment right to be free from unreasonable search and seizures. The police unreasonably seized him when they jailed him based on fabricated evidence, Manuel argued. The lower courts, however, dismissed Manuel's claim. The "Fourth Amendment falls out of the picture" once a judge looked at the case, the lower courts found. Manuel had brought his case under the wrong constitutional provision.

A 6–2 Supreme Court disagreed. The Fourth Amendment's protections remained in place even after a judge had looked into the case, the Court said. That amendment "prohibits government officials from detaining a person in the absence of probable cause," Justice Kagan wrote for the Court. "That can happen when the police hold someone without any reason before the formal onset of a criminal proceeding. But it also can occur when [the] legal process itself goes wrong—when, for example, a judge's probable-cause determination is predicated solely on a police officer's false statements." The Court reinstated Manuel's claim and sent it back to the lower courts determine if other procedural hurdles tripped up Manuel's case.

In addition to cases touching on race and the criminal justice system, the Court's division on criminal cases was evident in those dealing with the ability of citizens to hold government officials accountable for constitutional violations. The most consequential of those cases was sixteen years in the making, coming in the wake of the September 11, 2001, terrorist attacks. In the confusion that followed the attacks, the FBI received ninety-six thousand tips over a short period of time, the Supreme Court described. "Some tips were based on well-grounded suspicion of terrorist activity, but many others may have been based on fear of Arabs and Muslims," the Supreme Court explained. According to the plaintiffs' Supreme Court filings, "[One] of the original plaintiffs in this case 'came to the FBI's attention when his landlord called the FBI's 9/11 hotline and reported "that she rented an apartment in her home to several Middle Eastern men."'" The landlord said that "she would feel awful if her tenants were involved in terrorism and she didn't call."

Six noncitizens sued federal officials for the deplorable treatment they received while in custody—custody that lasted between three and eight months. The conditions of the confinement were "harsh," the Court said, recounting the allegations in the plaintiffs' lawsuit. They were held in "tiny cells" for twenty-three hours a day. When removed from these cells, they were "shackled and escorted by four guards." They were denied "communication with the outside world. And they were strip searched often—any time they were moved, as well as at random in their cells," the Supreme Court detailed. It went on to describe physical and verbal abuse directed at these detainees. "Guards allegedly slammed detainees into walls; twisted their arms, wrists, and fingers; broke their bones; referred to them as terrorists; threatened them with violence; subjected them to humiliating sexual comments; and insulted their religion."

If these facts were true, then what happened to the plaintiffs was "tragic," the Court said in its decision in *Ziglar v. Abbassi*. But while the Court did not condone such treatment, it found that the plaintiffs could not sue federal officials for money damages as recompense. The problem, in part, was that the plaintiffs sought to hold high-ranking government officials liable for their unconstitutional treatment. For example, they sued then FBI director Robert Mueller, who, just before the Supreme Court's decision in the case, had been tapped to lead the independent investigation into possible connection between the Trump campaign and Russian interference with the 2016 presidential election. In his role as FBI director, Mueller had ordered that each tip received by the FBI be investigated "even if the sole basis of 'suspicion' was the individual's religion, ethnicity, country of origin, or race," the plaintiffs claimed. Additionally, they sued former attorney general John Ashcroft and the head of the Immigration and Naturalization Service, who conspired to "round up every immigrant violator" who was a male between the ages of eighteen and forty and from a Middle Eastern country.

The issue for the Court was not whether such treatment was advisable or even constitutional, it explained. Instead, the issue was whether the Supreme Court was the correct venue to press such claims. It may come as a surprise to many that while federal law has for more than a hundred years provided a right for citizens to sue whenever a *state* official violates their constitutional rights, Congress has never provided that right when federal officials are the ones at fault. In the 1970s, the Supreme Court began inferring such a right. Known as a *Bivens* claim for the foundational case setting forth this right, the idea behind the Court's inference was that constitutional wrongs must have a way to be vindicated. After an initial period of expanding these *Bivens* claims, though, the Court began to contract the doctrine. The Court was "far more cautious" in inferring such a right now, the Supreme Court explained. Indeed, *Bivens* claims are now "disfavored."

In *Ziglar*, there were "special factors counseling hesitation" in allowing a *Bivens* action, the Court said. Allowing a cause of action in this and similar cases would "necessarily require inquiry and discovery into the whole course of the discussions and deliberations that led to the policies and governmental acts being challenged. . . . These consequences counsel against allowing a *Bivens* action against the Executive Officials, for the burden and demand of litigation might well prevent them—or, to be more precise, future officials like them—from devoting the time and effort required for the proper discharge of their duties." That could interfere with "sensitive functions of the Executive Branch," especially in the context of national security. Such judicial meddling in national security policy could "cause an official to second-guess difficult but necessary decisions," the Supreme Court concluded.

The Court's *Ziglar* decision had a curious vote count, coming down 4–2. Justice Sotomayor had been involved with the case when she was an appellate court judge on the Second Circuit. Justice Kagan had been the solicitor general while it was actively working its way through the federal courts. Justice Gorsuch, of course, had not yet been confirmed to the bench when *Ziglar* was argued. The remaining six justices that participated were the bare minimum that the Court could have and still consider a case. If there were fewer, the decision below would be habitually affirmed. Justice Breyer wrote for the two justices in dissent—himself and Justice Ginsburg. He agreed that a *Bivens* action in this context could provide some troublesome complications. But the courts had developed protections for federal officials that could address those concerns, Justice Breyer argued. "If you are cold, put on a sweater, perhaps an overcoat, perhaps also turn up the heat, but do not set fire to the house." On the other side of the scale, history "tells us of far too many instances where the Executive or Legislative Branch took actions during time of war that, on later examination, turned out unnecessarily and unreasonably to have deprived American citizens of basic constitutional rights," Breyer went on to say. He pointed to the "thousands of civilians imprisoned during the Civil War," the "suppression of civil liberties during World War I," and the Supreme Court's blessing of the removal of "more than 70,000 American citizens of Japanese origin from their west coast homes" to be interned in camps.

Perhaps the Court's result in *Ziglar* should have been clear to court watchers following the unanimous decision in *County of Los Angeles v. Mendez.* There, the Court overturned a $4 million award in favor of a homeless couple shot by Los Angeles police. One of the pair was pregnant at the time of the shooting; the other was crippled as a result of it. The officers had entered their shack without a warrant and without announcing themselves as police. The Supreme Court's decision in that case did not turn on whether the plaintiffs could sue the officials, but rather on a quirky rule from the Ninth Circuit that made it easier for plaintiffs to prove the substance of their claims. Known as the "provocation rule," it turned an officer's reasonable use of force into an unreasonable use if the officer had provoked the need for force. The officer here had provoked the use of force by failing to get a warrant, the Ninth Circuit said. The provocation rule itself was "incompatible" with the Court's previous case law, the Supreme Court believed. Unreasonable force was to be judged "from the perspective of a reasonable officer on the scene," not the "20/20 vision of hindsight," the Court said, quoting from its earlier cases. By looking far back into the past to the failure to get a warrant, the Ninth Circuit "uses another constitutional violation to manufacture an excessive force claim where one would not otherwise exist."

While *Mendez's* consequences on *Ziglar* may have been obscured, *Ziglar's* significance to another "tragic" case was obvious. In 2010, US Border Patrol agent Jesus Mesa Jr. shot across the US border at fifteen-year-old Mexican national Sergio Adrián Hernández Güereca. "One shot struck Hernández in the face and killed him," the Supreme Court would ultimately say in its opinion in a case brought by Hernández's family against Mesa. According to the family, the incident occurred during a game Hernández had been playing with his friends, in which they would race to the US border and back. Based on those facts, the Mexican government charged Mesa with murder and sought to try him in their courts. But the Justice Department determined that Mesa only fatally shot Hernández after the teen had unsuccessfully attempted to illegally cross the border and subsequently threw rocks at Mesa while the agent attempted to apprehend one of Hernández's accomplices. The United States, therefore, refused to extradite Mesa to Mexico to face murder charges.

Given the "procedural posture" of the case, the Supreme Court credited Hernández's family's account of the events. Because Mesa was attempting to nix the case before it even went to trial, the Supreme Court asked whether the facts alleged by the Hernández family could ever entitle them to relief against Mesa. Unable to get relief in their own country, the family sought to hold Mesa accountable under two sections of the US Constitution. First, the family argued that Mesa had violated the Fourth Amendment's prohibition against unreasonable seizures by killing Hernández without justification. While the Fourth Amendment may protect an American on foreign soil or a foreign national on American soil, it clearly did not reach across the border to protect a Mexican national, the en banc Fifth Circuit said. Next, the Hernández family claimed that Mesa's excessive use of force violated the Fifth Amendment's due process clause. The Fifth Circuit was "somewhat divided" on whether the Fifth Amendment protected Hernández as a foreign national on foreign soil, but they unanimously agreed that Mesa was entitled to "qualified immunity" on such a claim. The doctrine of qualified immunity protects state officials from having to defend against allegations that they violated an individual's constitutional rights, so long as the official did not violate "clearly established" rights. As evidenced by the division on between the Fifth Circuit judges, it was not clearly established that the Fifth Amendment reached across the border to protect Hernández, the judges declared.

The Supreme Court, though, bounced the case back to the Fifth Circuit for reconsideration of an issue that the parties had not asked the high court to address. When agreeing to hear a case, the Supreme Court will occasionally add to or modify the questions that the parties have asked the Court to address. Here, the Court told the parties that in addition to deciding whether the Fourth Amendment applied extraterritorially and if Mesa was entitled to qualified immunity on the Fifth Amendment claim, it would consider if the Hernández family could even bring its Fourth and Fifth Amendment claims under *Bivens.* When the Court finally handed down its decision in *Hernández* on the last day of its term, it gently chided the Fifth Circuit for skipping over the *Bivens* question and instead proceeding to decide whether the Fourth Amendment applied across the border to a Mexican national. "This approach—disposing of a *Bivens* claim by resolving the constitutional question, while assuming the existence of a *Bivens* remedy—is appropriate in many cases," the Supreme Court said. But not here. The Fourth Amendment question in this case was "sensitive and may have consequence that are far reaching. It would be imprudent for this Court to resolve that issue when, in light of the intervening guidance provided" in *Ziglar v. Abbassi,* "doing so may be unnecessary to resolve this particular case." The Court, however, did not want to decide the *Bivens* question itself either. As Ian Samuel, cohost of the Supreme Court podcast *First Mondays,* put it, after inserting the question into the case, hearing briefing and argument, the justices decided they did not want to decide the *Bivens* question after all. "We want you to do it first," Samuel described the justices' response to the Fifth Circuit.

So the justices sent Hernández's family back to the Fifth Circuit to see if its *Bivens* claim could fare any better than the detainees' claim in *Ziglar v. Abbassi.* But the Court also took part of the qualified immunity question off the Fifth Circuit's plate. There was not a clearly established right of Fifth Amendment protection to a foreign national across the US border, but those facts—in particular, Hernández's connection to the United States—were not known to Mesa at the time that he shot at the teen. Qualified immunity was to be determined based on the facts known to the officer at the time, the Court declared. "Facts an officer learns after the incident ends—whether those facts would support granting immunity or denying it—are not relevant."

While the members of the Court generally seemed to be on the same page regarding qualified immunity in *Hernández*, the Court's division on this issue would be laid bare on what University of Chicago Law School professor William Baude calls the Court's "shadow docket." The justices' most reported-on work comes from its shrinking merits docket. These are the high court cases that most of us think of when imagining the Court at work: a sixty-minute oral argument followed by a thorough, pages-long majority opinion, regularly trailed with an entertaining and well-reasoned dissenting view. But the Court is regularly asked to act on "applications" ranging from matters as mundane as an essentially automatic extension of time to file a cert petition to those as consequential as a stay of execution. Along with these applications are the seven to eight thousand petitions for certiorari that the Supreme Court is asked to consider. The justices infrequently explain their votes in these matters, let alone the reasons animating those decisions. It would be a Herculean task for justices to explain their reasonings in the thousands of cases brought before them. So when they take the effort to write an explanation of a particular decision, it is because they want someone to know. Justice Sotomayor's powerful dissent from the Court's refusal to hear another qualified immunity case from the Fifth Circuit seemed to fit that bill.

In 2010, Houston officer Chris Thompson shot Ricardo Salazar-Limon in the back after a confrontation in which Thompson unsuccessfully tried to handcuff him. Salazar-Limon claims that as soon as he broke away from Thompson, the officer shot him in the back, resulting in paralyzing injuries. Thompson, however, says he only shot Salazar-Limon after he reached for his waistband, seemingly to grab a weapon. Yet Salazar-Limon was never found to have such a weapon. The question of whether Thompson was entitled to qualified immunity, thus saving him from having to go to trial, or if he instead had used unconstitutional force when shooting Salazar-Limon turned "in large part on which man is telling the truth," Justice Sotomayor stated. "Our legal system entrusts this decision to a jury sitting as finder of fact, not a judge reviewing a paper record." The district court below had done just the opposite in resolving the case in favor of the officer. But the "evenhanded administration of justice does not permit such a shortcut," Sotomayor said.

Justice Alito, joined by Justice Thomas, acknowledged that Justice Sotomayor's conclusion about who was telling the truth—namely, that the district court could not really tell—"is surely debatable." But, he went on, every "year courts of appeals decide hundreds of cases in which they must determine whether thin evidence provided by a plaintiff is just enough to survive" or "not quite enough." The Supreme Court does not usually grant cert in these numerous cases to resolve such factual questions, Alito explained. The courts have no way of knowing what really happened that night. "All that the lower courts and this

Court can do is to apply the governing rules in a neutral fashion." Because the lower court did that, the Supreme Court was right to turn away Salazar-Limon's case, Alito concluded.

That, however, did not sit well with Justice Sotomayor. The Court's refusal to correct the error "continues a disturbing trend regarding the use of this Court's resources. We have not hesitated to summarily reverse courts for wrongly denying officers the protection of qualified immunity in cases involving the use of force," Sotomayor explained. "But we rarely intervene where courts wrongly afford officers the benefit of qualified immunity in these same cases. The erroneous grant of summary judgment in qualified-immunity cases imposes no less harm on [society] . . . than does the erroneous denial of summary judgment in such cases." The Court had taken steps "toward addressing this asymmetry" in the past, she said. "We take one step back today."

It seems clear that qualified immunity will emerge as a point of tension in future terms. But one of the fiercest battles that has raged in the Supreme Court over the past few terms has also played out largely on the Court's shadow docket: the constitutionality of the death penalty. The dispute, however, did not start there. Instead, the Court's division over this controversial issue was exposed in an argued case decided on the last day of the Supreme Court's 2014 term. In *Glossip v. Gross*, the Court considered death row inmates' challenge to Oklahoma's three-drug cocktail used for carrying out lethal injections. The first drug was used to sedate the prisoner, the second paralyzed him, and the third stopped his heart. Due to what Justice Alito called a guerilla war embarked on by death penalty abolitionists, states were having a hard time coming by the first of these drugs, as foreign companies were pressured to refuse to sell the drug for use in administering capital punishment. Oklahoma, along with other states, was therefore forced to rely on a less reliable drug (midazolam) to render the prisoner unconscious. The challenge to the use of this drug was based largely on the botched execution of Clayton Lockett. The confessed rapist and killer's painful execution was rivetingly detailed by *The Atlantic's* Jeffrey E. Stern, who described the unusually long (nearly sixty-minute) procedure. To begin with, the executioners had difficulty inserting the IV needed to deliver the lethal drugs. Lockett was "stuck with needles more than a dozen times" before they were able to get the IV properly in place, Stern described. Or so they thought. The IV had actually dislodged. The result was that the drugs did not work properly to sedate and paralyze Lockett, so that he writhed and convulsed from the excruciating final drug.

Following Lockett's execution, Charles Warner, Richard Glossip, and other Oklahoma inmates set to die by the same three-drug cocktail challenged the procedure as cruel and unusual punishment in violation of the Eighth Amendment. After refusing to stop Warner's execution, the Supreme Court later decided to hear the challenge. Richard Glossip became the lead plaintiff because Warner had been executed by the time the Court heard oral argument. The case, however, would not end up saving Glossip either (though later stays of execution would). That was because the Supreme Court decided 5–4 that the death row inmates could not challenge the current procedure without putting forth "a known and available alternative method of execution that entails a lesser risk of pain" before they could proceed with their claims. The prisoners had not done that, and so their executions could go forward.

A summary of the decision, like every other Supreme Court opinion, was read from the bench by the opinion's author—here, Justice Alito. Occasionally, dissenting justices will also read parts of their dissents from the bench, but they generally save such theatrics for when they vehemently disagree. Justice Sotomayor was the only one of two justices to do that during the Court's 2016 term, when she read her fiery dissent in *Trinity Lutheran*. In 2014, Sotomayor also decided that *Glossip* necessitated an oral rebuke. Oddly, though, Justice Breyer also decided to read from his dissenting opinion in *Glossip*. In the five terms that I have covered the Court, I have never seen or heard of more than one justice reading a dissent from the bench on the same case. Justice Breyer's dissent, however, was a comprehensive denunciation of the death penalty as currently carried out. "Today's administration of the death penalty involves three fundamental constitutional defects," Justice Breyer wrote in his dissent. "(1) serious unreliability, (2) arbitrariness in application, and (3) unconscionably long delays that undermine the death penalty's penological purpose." He described each of these defects in painstaking detail in a forty-one-page opinion. These shortcomings, "taken together with [his] own 20 years of experience on this Court," led Justice Breyer to conclude that the death penalty was likely unconstitutional. "[Rather] than try to patch up the death penalty's legal wounds one at a time, I would ask for full briefing on a more basic question: whether the death penalty violates the Constitution," Justice Breyer declared.

Remarkably, the Court's session was not done with Justice Breyer's reading. Justice Scalia, who had concurred with the result in *Glossip*, also decided to read his opinion from the bench in order to address Justice Breyer's extraordinary claims. The Court does not publicly make available the justices' bench statements, but Scalia's written decision conveys the hostility with which he viewed Justice Breyer's assertions. "Capital punishment presents moral questions that philosophers, theologians, and statesmen have grappled with for millennia," Scalia wrote. Because our nation's founders "disagreed bitterly on the matter. . . . they left it to the People to decide. By arrogating to himself the power to overturn that decision, Justice Breyer does not just reject the death penalty, he rejects the Enlightenment," Scalia scolded.

The fierce disagreement over the constitutionality of the death penalty continued two terms after *Glossip*. Though the Court has so far declined to take on Justice Breyer's invitation to reassess the death penalty as a whole, the Court has considered the issue piecemeal, dealing with narrow aspects of capital sentencing. One such case during the Court's 2016 term was *McWilliams v. Dunn*. The issue for the Court here was if indigent capital defendants were entitled to a mental health expert who was separate from the prosecution and could provide assistance to the defense or if, instead, the mental health expert had to simply be neutral. Alabama determined that it was the latter, and McWilliams appealed after being sentenced to death following the denial of his counsel's request for another mental health expert. An overwhelming majority of states, though, had read their responsibility to provide a mental health expert more broadly, so the issue in *McWilliams* had an exceedingly limited application.

The case, however, would take on more significance after Arkansas's announcement of "assembly-line executions." The last time Arkansas had executed someone was in 2005. But in early 2017, the state said it would execute eight death-row inmates over eleven days, with executions proceeding back-to-back on several days. The hurry for Arkansas was based on an expiration date. The state's supply of the controversial and hard-to-acquire drug midazolam, which had been the subject of the Court's *Glossip* decision, was about to expire. The prospects were not good that the state could acquire more. All of the capital defendants facing imminent execution sought to halt those executions via the governor, lower state and federal courts, and/or the US Supreme Court. Several were successful in putting off their executions, including two who received last-minute stays from the Arkansas Supreme Court. The defendants in those cases asserted similar claims as McWilliams. The executions were put on hold until the US Supreme Court decided the demands of the Constitution.

With this heightened importance, a nine-member Supreme Court heard *McWilliams v. Dunn* in April 2017. When the Court handed down its decision on June 19, it was the first 5–4 decision since Justice Scalia's death in February 2016. It was also Justice Gorsuch's first public dissenting vote as a Supreme Court justice, joining Chief Justice Roberts and Justices Thomas and Alito in dissent. The majority found, in an opinion by Justice Breyer, that "when certain threshold criteria are met, the State must provide an indigent defendant with access to a mental health expert who is sufficiently available to the defense and independent from the prosecution to effectively 'assist in evaluation, preparation, and presentation of the defense.'"

Similar division over the death penalty was seen in *Moore v. Texas*, another narrow challenge to the death penalty. In 2002, the Supreme Court declared that it violated the Eighth Amendment's prohibition against cruel and unusual punishment to execute mentally disabled individuals. "Because of their disabilities in areas of reasoning, judgment, and control of their impulses . . . [mentally disabled criminals] do not act with the level of moral culpability that characterizes the most serious adult criminal conduct," the Court said in *Atkins v. Virginia*. In the ensuing years, a rash of cases reached the Court regarding the mechanism for determining when a capital defendant qualified as mentally disabled. *Moore* was one such case. Texas had based its determination that Moore was mentally fit to be executed on unreliable standards that failed to take into account the "medical community's diagnostic framework," the Court said. Unsurprisingly, the decision was decided along ideological lines, with Justice Kennedy joining the Court's more liberal bloc; the three more conservative justices dissented.

These two cases, plus the Court's decision in *Buck*, showcased the justices' disagreement on several aspects of the death penalty. But the remainder of the Court's wrangling on this topic occurred on the Court's murky shadow docket. Moreover, the division among the justices played out not just between liberals and conservatives but also between the liberals themselves. In a series of requests following *Glossip*, the liberal justices cast their votes seemingly inconsistently in deciding whether to stay executions. While they occasionally voted together, Justice Breyer often was the lone dissent from the Court's refusal to halt an impending execution. Justices Ginsburg and Sotomayor, to a lesser degree, also were lone dissenters in such cases. The inconsistency could evince that these justices were struggling with how to respond to growing public unease with the death penalty, William Baude speculated. "[It] could also be that they are simply being selective in which cases they want to highlight, perhaps choosing the ones they think will be the most sympathetic."

That theory seemed to hold water during the 2016 term. For example, Justice Breyer has highlighted so-called *Lackey* claims by writing dissents from the Supreme Court's refusal to address the constitutionality of prolonged imprisonment on death row. He was the sole dissent in *Sireci v. Florida*, involving the 1976 conviction and death sentence of Henry Sireci. "[Sireci] has lived in prison under threat of execution for 40 years," Breyer detailed. "When he was first sentenced to death, the Berlin Wall stood firmly in place. Saigon had just fallen. Few Americans knew of the personal computer or the Internet. And over half of all Americans now alive had not yet been born. . . . [Given that the] uncertainty before execution is 'one of the most horrible feelings to which [a prisoner] can be subjected,'" such delay violates the Eighth Amendment, Breyer professed. Not a single other justice signed on to his opinion.

Justice Sotomayor seems to have a similar interest in so-called method claims—those cases, like *Glossip*, that challenge the method of execution. In *Arthur v. Dunn*,

Justice Sotomayor dissented from the Court's refusal to honor Thomas Arthur's request to be executed via firing squad rather than via legal injection using midazolam. Lower courts had turned Arthur away because he had not met *Glossip*'s command to identify a "known and alternative" method of execution. Firing squad was not permitted by Alabama's capital punishment statutes and thus was not "available," the lower courts said. Justice Sotomayor found that "macabre challenge" to be constitutionally suspect. It allowed the state "to immunize their methods of execution—no matter how cruel or how unusual—from judicial review and thus permits state law to subvert the Federal Constitution['s prohibition against cruel and unusual punishment.]" Epitomizing the problems with the shadow docket, there was no response to either Justice Breyer's dissent in *Sireci* or Justice Sotomayor's in *Arthur*, leaving the American public to only guess where the other justices stand on this life-and-death issue.

Calm before the Storm

Court watchers commonly say that a new justice can change the entire dynamic of the Court. After all, there are only nine justices on the US Supreme Court. Many think, though, that Justice Gorsuch will be similar to his iconic predecessor. To begin with, Justice Gorsuch is an admirer of the late Justice Scalia. After Scalia's death, but before he was nominated as his successor, Justice Gorsuch described him as "a lion of the law: docile in private life but a ferocious fighter when at work, with a roar that could echo for miles." He recounted the moment he heard of Justice Scalia's death: "I was taking a breather in the middle of a ski run with little on my mind but the next mogul field when my phone rang with the news. I immediately lost what breath I had left, and I am not embarrassed to admit that I couldn't see the rest of the way down the mountain for the tears." This vivid—if also dramatic—style is reminiscent of Justice Scalia, whose sharp dissents would often catch headlines. By all accounts, however, Justice Gorsuch is a more reserved individual. He is Justice Scalia "without the rough edges," the Cato Institute's Ilya Shapiro described him.

That genteel nature was on display during his seemingly marathon Senate confirmation hearing in late March 2017. The soon-to-be justice was visibly taken aback at the start of the hearing when dozens of cameras clicked and snapped frame after frame of the previously under-the-radar judge. Then judge Gorsuch turned away from the spotlight to his friends and family in the audience and made a cringing facial expression, as if to say, "This is wild." Folksy mannerisms like this seemed out of place at the center of such a classically partisan, Washingtonian battle. Phrases like "gosh," "golly," and "for goodness' sake" were uttered by the nominee on more than one occasion.

But his down-home style did not deflect the ire of Senate Democrats still seething over their colleagues' treatment of Merrick Garland. Republicans on the Judiciary Committee tried to head off some of the intense questioning that would befall Judge Gorsuch. The role of the Judiciary Committee was not to ensure that the nominee shared the beliefs of the committee members, they argued. Instead, the Senate was limited to assessing Judge Gorsuch's qualifications. With two Ivy League degrees, an advanced degree from Oxford, a stint in the White House, and nearly a decade on the federal appellate bench, it was hard to poke holes in Judge Gorsuch's credentials. The confirmation process clearly was not about qualifications, Democrats countered. If that were the case, Judge Merrick Garland would now be Justice Garland, they pointed out. Democrats were therefore free to probe Judge Gorsuch to ensure that his principles aligned with that of mainstream Americans.

Democrats, though, did not like what they discovered. In a somewhat forced attempt to paint Judge Gorsuch as favoring big business and opposing the "little guy," Democrats hammered Gorsuch over a 2016 case that would become known simply as the Frozen Trucker Case. In the late hours of a cold winter day in 2009, trucker Alphonse Maddin's trailer brakes froze up. His employer told him to either drag the trailer back to the shop or stay there and wait for help. Faced with these two options—one unsafe, the other unpleasant—Maddin stayed put . . . for hours. Eventually, feeling unwell from the subzero temperatures, Maddin unhooked his trailer and drove to warmth. His employer later fired him for not following orders.

Judge Gorsuch was one of three judges who heard Maddin's appeal. The two justices in the majority agreed with the Department of Labor that Maddin could not be fired for his actions. Gorsuch, though, dissented. "It might be fair to ask whether [the employer's] decision was a wise or kind one," Judge Gorsuch wrote. "But it's not our job to answer questions like that. Our only task is to decide whether the decision was an illegal one," Gorsuch declared. He determined that the decision was legal. Democrats would point to this case often during the four-day-long hearing as an example of Gorsuch twisting the law to rule in favor of corporations rather than people. The weather Maddin faced was cold, Democratic Senator Richard Durbin said. But "not as cold as your dissent," he told Gorsuch.

It did not help that Judge Gorsuch refused to answer almost any substantive questions asked by Senate Democrats. When asked about what Democratic Senator Dianne Feinstein called the abortion "super precedent," Judge Gorsuch invoked the "Ginsburg rule." Coined by conservatives in reference to Justice Ginsburg's confirmation hearing, the idea is that a judicial nominee should not express an opinion about a matter that might come before him or her while on the bench. Such a rule is intended to protect the integrity of the judicial system and make later parties feel as though they have gotten a fair shake. But Judge Gorsuch seemed to take this "rule" to the extreme. "You have been very much able to avoid any specificity like no one I have ever seen before," stated longtime Judiciary Committee member Feinstein disapprovingly. Even Chief Justice Roberts and Justice Alito answered *some* questions about the Court's prior cases at their confirmation hearings, Senator Patrick Leahy noted.

The Supreme Court itself made Judge Gorsuch's task of winning over Democrats more difficult. Right in the middle of his confirmation hearing, the Court issued a unanimous rebuke of the way Gorsuch's former court—the Tenth Circuit—had interpreted the responsibilities of public schools toward disabled students. What followed was one of the few times during Judge Gorsuch's hours of testimony that his polite veneer seemed to crack and his distaste for the process showed through.

The Individuals with Disabilities Education Act (IDEA) requires that public schools provide disabled students with a "free appropriate public education." In 1982, the Supreme Court unhelpfully explained that that phrase required schools to provide "some educational benefit." The Supreme Court did not return to the IDEA's free, appropriate, public education requirement until the 2016 term in *Endrew F. v. Douglas County School District RE-1*. Given the Supreme Court's vague clarification, it was no surprise that the lower federal courts had come to different determinations of what the law required. The Tenth Circuit—from which both the *Endrew F.* case and Gorsuch came—had read the law's requirements quite narrowly: The school must provide educational benefits that are "merely more than de minimus." During oral argument in *Endrew F.*, the justices seemed troubled by this phrasing—especially the term "merely," the *Huffington Post*'s Cristian Farias pointed out. The standard "sounds very harsh," Justice Alito said. "Who thought this up?" "Who put the term, 'more than merely de minimus?'" Justice Ginsburg interjected. "And de minimus is not enough, you know," Justice Kagan added. "It's 'merely de minimus.'"

Several days before Gorsuch's confirmation hearing, the Supreme Court had announced that it would issue opinions on some of the days that their soon-to-be-colleague would be appearing before the Judiciary Committee. They did not, however, disclose which cases they would decide. So at ten a.m. on March 22, as Gorsuch was undergoing his final day of testimony, the Supreme Court handed down its unanimous decision to overturn Gorsuch's former court in *Endrew F.* To make matters worse, it was an opinion by the Court's most senior member, the chief justice. The appropriate standard for determining when the IDEA's promise of a "free appropriate public education" will often turn on unique facts specific to the case at hand. "But whatever else can be said about it, this standard is markedly more demanding than the 'merely more than *de minimus*' test applied by the Tenth Circuit."

Now, Judge Gorsuch was not one of the judges who considered *Endrew F.* when the case was in the Tenth Circuit. And *Endrew F.* was based on a 1996 decision that established the rule in the Tenth Circuit as "more than de minimus." Judge Gorsuch was not a part of that decision either. But Judge Gorsuch had been the one to later insert the phrase "merely" into the Tenth Circuit's IDEA standard, according to Senator Durbin. By inserting the word "merely" into an already weak standard, Judge Gorsuch had pushed the de minimus standard "even further down the standard pole," Durbin said. Given Gorsuch's refusal to answer substantive questions, senators had to examine Judge Gorsuch's judicial opinion to "try to look into [his] heart" to see what kind of justice Gorsuch would be. Again invoking frozen trucker Maddin's case, Durbin suggested that what he saw made Gorsuch unfit to be a Supreme Court justice.

But Judge Gorsuch was charming during his confirmation hearing too—indeed, more frequently endearing than unpleasant. He had an enjoyably confounding exchange with Republican Senator Jeff Flake over questions the senator's family had texted in to ask: Would the judge rather fight a hundred duck-sized horses or one horse-sized duck? Flake's teenage son wanted to know. Judge Gorsuch entertainingly described to Republican Senator Ted Cruz his advice to his two girls about "mutton busting"— the rodeo tradition of having children ride sheep. Most memorably, Judge Gorsuch appeared genuinely embarrassed by an exchange with Republican Senator Ben Sasse over the importance of the Declaration of Independence. The document was a "death warrant," Judge Gorsuch said. The high stakes made the signatories of the Declaration of Independence iconic. He highlighted John Hancock as someone that everyone affiliates with a signature. That was because Hancock signed the Declaration of Independence so "bigly," Gorsuch mistakenly said. While trying to clarify that he meant so "big and boldly," Senator Sasse joked that Gorsuch had just used a Trumpism frequently discussed during the 2016 election. More ink than was probably necessary had been spilt during that election over then candidate Trump's use of the phrase "bigly" (or, perhaps, "big league"). Gorsuch admitted to being embarrassed by the slip up and even struggled to regain his footing.

Eventually, though, Justice Gorsuch was confirmed after a bitter battle that resulted in historic change to the confirmation process for Supreme Court justices. Known as the "nuclear option," the Republicans jettisoned the once-impenetrable filibuster for Supreme Court nominees that essentially required a minimum level of bipartisan support. That drastic step seemed inevitable after Senate Democrats ditched the procedure for all judicial nominees except those to the Supreme Court in 2013. If Gorsuch had not been the nominee, the same result was likely to have occurred. Still, the discourse surrounding Justice Gorsuch's confirmation battle is sure to have changed the tenor and outcome of the Supreme Court confirmation process going forward.

Following that dramatic and consequential fight, Justice Gorsuch quickly took his seat on April 10 and prepared for impending oral arguments, which began just a week later. During that sitting, the justices considered thirteen cases, most of which Justice Gorsuch vigorously participated in. It is too soon to judge a justice only months into what could conceivably be upward of three decades on the Supreme Court. But those thirteen cases, and several others in which Justice Gorsuch went out of his way to weigh in on, laid markers for what to expect in the future.

First, in the footsteps of his predecessor, Justice Gorsuch has expressed a strong inclination toward textualism—

deferring to the text of a statute in determining its meaning. Indeed, Justice Gorsuch's first opinion on the high court bench was a statutory interpretation case over the reach of consumer protection laws. In *Henson v. Santander Consumer USA Inc.*, Justice Gorsuch questioned Congress's logic in drawing debt protection lines where it did. But "the proper role of the judiciary . . . [is] to apply, not amend, the work of the People's representatives," Justice Gorsuch wrote.

While all justices look to some extent at the words Congress uses in passing laws, Justice Gorsuch seems ready to follow that text where his colleagues might find it appropriate to look for meaning elsewhere. Take *Perry v. Merits Systems Protection Board*, a case involving a complex statutory scheme meant to deal with employment complaints by federal employees. In particular, the case sought to sort out where certain cases went once dismissed by the federal Merit Systems Protection Board—to the federal district courts or the courts of appeals. Ultimately, the Supreme Court said that they should go first to the district court. But during oral argument—Gorsuch's first as a Supreme Court justice—the rookie took issue with an ancillary question that both parties and federal courts—including the Supreme Court—have agreed on for decades. Gorsuch, though, did not think the statute actually said that and did not want the Supreme Court "just to continue to make it up." "Wouldn't it be a lot easier if we just followed the plain text of the statute?" Justice Gorsuch asked. Justice Alito—likely to become one of Justice Gorsuch's closest allies on the bench—did not see the text as all that easy to decipher. "The one thing about this case that seems perfectly clear to me is that nobody who is not a lawyer and no ordinary lawyer could read these statutes and figure out what they are supposed to do," Alito said to laughter. "Who wrote this statute? Somebody who takes pleasure out of pulling the wings off flies?" Alito quipped. Justice Kagan, too, pointed out that Justice Gorsuch's interpretation "would be a kind of revolution" in this area of the law. Gorsuch, though, did not back down. In his first written dissent as a Supreme Court justice, Gorsuch wrote, "At the end of a long day, I just cannot find anything preventing us from applying the statute as written—or heard any good reason for deviating from its terms. . . . The only thing that seems sure to follow from [the majority's decision] is all the time and money litigants will spend, and all the ink courts will spill, as they work their way to a wholly remodeled statutory regime. Respectfully, Congress already wrote a perfectly good law. I would follow it."

The second marker that Justice Gorsuch laid during his short time on the bench during the 2016 term was that he would not shy away from acting on his opinions or fail to make his preferences known. New justices are often said to take a few years to get into the full swing of the awesome responsibilities of being a Supreme Court justice. For Gorsuch, the lead time was more like a few days. That was most notable on the Court's final day of the 2016 term. Although the closing day is often a time for fireworks at the Court, the Court's docket this term did not have any blockbusters. The day, though, was made more exciting by Gorsuch's unexpected flood of opinions. First, he wrote to explain why he would or would not have granted cert in three cases that the Supreme Court either turned away or acted on summarily. In cases on the Takings Clause, criminal sentencing, and the Office of Veterans' Affairs, Justice Gorsuch went out of his way to make his opinions known to the American public. He also penned a concurring opinion in the term's closest analogue to a blockbuster—*Trinity Lutheran*.

Perhaps the most notable opinion handed down by Justice Gorsuch on the term's final day came in *Pavan v. Smith*, a case that tested the reach of the Supreme Court's landmark same-sex marriage ruling in 2015. In particular, although Arkansas required that married opposite-sex couples both be included on their child's birth certificate, the state prohibited both married same-sex couples from appearing on the vital document. For medical reasons, it was advantageous to link children with their biological parents, the state proffered. Those rules, however, were similar even where the child was conceived via artificial insemination. A married opposite-sex spouse would be on such a baby's birth certificate. A married same-sex spouse in the same situation would not. Three Arkansas couples challenged the law, but they were turned away by the Arkansas Supreme Court. The US Supreme Court in *Obergefell* declared that "the right to marry is a fundamental right inherent in the liberty of the person" that cannot constitutionally be deprived. In the Arkansas Supreme Court's view, the question in *Pavan* did not "concern either the right to same-sex marriage or the recognition of that marriage. . . . What is before this court is the narrow issue of whether the birth-certificate statutes as written deny the appellees due process." Having focused the inquiry onto that narrow issue, the Arkansas Supreme Court was easily able to uphold the state's birth-certificate scheme. "*Obergefell* did not address Arkansas's statutory framework regarding birth certificates, either expressly or impliedly." The issue, therefore, was left up to the states.

Arkansas, though, was an outlier. Every other court to have considered similar laws had determined that the law had to be applied in a gender-neutral way to accommodate same-sex couples, according to Supreme Court papers filed by the couples challenging Arkansas's law. "On the whole," states that refused to recognize same-sex marriages prior to *Obergefell* "fell in line" after the decision to provide same-sex couples with equal treatment, according to the couples' attorney, Douglas Hallward-Driemeier, who had argued in support of same-sex marriage in *Obergefell* itself. But there were some holdouts. He pointed to a case during the Court's 2015 term in which an adoption by a same-sex couple was undone when the Alabama Supreme Court refused to recognize the adoption during the couple's divorce. *Obergefell* did not apply to adoption, the state court had determined. The Supreme Court had summarily, and unanimously, reversed that decision. The decision had relied on another constitutional question not decided—but considered—in *Obergefell*. Still, the summary action by the Court showed that even if there was disagreement over the constitutionality of laws prohibiting same-sex marriage, there was not any over whether states could ignore that decision, Hallward-Driemeier said.

The Supreme Court—without hearing oral argument in the case—summarily overturned the Arkansas Supreme Court's decision in *Pavan*. "As we explained [in *Obergefell*], a State may not 'exclude same-sex couples from civil marriage on the same terms and conditions as opposite-sex couples.'" The Court had even specifically identified "birth and death certificates" as one those terms and conditions. "That was no accident: Several of the plaintiffs in *Obergefell* challenged a State's refusal to recognize their same-sex spouses on their children's birth certificates." *Obergefell* found such "laws unconstitutional to the extent they treated same-sex couples differently from opposite-sex couples," the Court said in its unsigned opinion. "That holding applies with equal force to [Arkansas' birth certificate law.]"

Justice Gorsuch's dissent, joined by Justices Thomas and Alito, explained that such summary action was typically reserved for when the court below "clearly" erred in applying well-settled law. "To be sure, *Obergefell* addressed the question whether a State must recognize same-sex marriages," Justice Gorsuch acknowledged. "But nothing in Obergefell spoke (let alone clearly) to the question whether [Arkansas' birth certificate statute], or a state supreme court decision upholding it, must go." Moreover, the law's most basic gender distinction could be justified by "reasons that in no way offend *Obergefell*," Justice Gorsuch said—that is, ensuring government officials can identify public health trends and helping individuals determine their biological lineage, citizenship, or susceptibility to genetic disorders. The majority did not explain why such a biology-based distinction is counter to the Constitution, Justice Gorsuch pointed out. The offensive part of the statute, Justice Gorsuch guessed, was what he called the statute's "exceptions"—namely, the provision regarding birth registry for artificial insemination. Arkansas had already conceded that the exception must be applied on a gender-neutral basis, according to Justice Gorsuch. It was not clear, therefore, "what the Court expects to happen on remand that hasn't happened already. The Court does not offer any remedial suggestion, and none leaps to mind. Perhaps the state supreme court could memorialize the State's concession" regarding the artificial insemination provision, Gorsuch suggested, even though "such a chore is hardly the usual reward for seeking faithfully to apply, not evade, this Court's mandates."

Justice Gorsuch's willingness to confront such controversial issues stands in sharp contrast to the Court's approach during the rest of the 2016 term. That points to a return to the spotlight for the Supreme Court in the coming years. In addition to hearing the challenge to President Trump's travel ban, the Court will tackle during its 2017 term the explosive issue of religious exemptions from antidiscrimination laws in *Masterpiece Cakeshop, Ltd. v. Colorado Civil Rights Commission*. The latter is the latest example of a wedding service provider being sued because it refused to make its services available for same-sex weddings. *Masterpiece Cakeshop* involves a baker, but other cases have involved photographers and florists. The gist of the argument is that that forcing business owners to provide services for ceremonies that violate their religious beliefs seriously impinges on religious freedom. Here, Masterpiece Cakeshop owner Jack C. Phillips said he would have baked any other goods for Charlie Craig and David Mullins—just not a wedding cake. The problem for Phillips is that Colorado prohibits businesses from discriminating against patrons "because of" their sexual orientation. Phillips countered that he did not discriminate against Craig and Mullins "because of" their sexual orientation, but rather "because of" their conduct—namely, participating in a same-sex wedding. That distinction was "one without a difference," a Colorado court found. In addition to prohibiting the shop from engaging in similar discrimination in the future, the bakery was required to file quarterly reports on its compliance.

Chapter 8

Phillips filed his petition for certiorari in the US Supreme Court in July 2016. The case was first considered by the justices in their private conference at the end of September. Following that conference, the justices asked the state commission—which had initially found Phillips in violation of the state's antidiscrimination law—to respond to Phillips's request. Once the commission had filed its reasons for the Supreme Court to let the lower court's decision stand, the Supreme Court again considered the case at a private conference. Following that conference, the justices again asked for more information. This time they requested the lower court to send over the "record"—that is, the facts and evidence that the court had relied on in making its decision. The Supreme Court received that record in January 2017, and then . . . nothing. For six months, the Court considered the case in fifteen separate conferences where, presumably, the justices discussed only whether to set the case for argument and consider the case in full. It is unclear what held up the justices' decision in the case. Perhaps the Court was hesitant to step into this divisive issue without the input from the soon-to-be-appointed ninth justice. Perhaps the Court had decided not to take the case and someone was writing a brutal dissent from that decision. No one will know for sure for decades, as the justices' private papers detailing such issues are not made public until long after their deaths. What I do know is that on the last day of the 2016 term, the justices agreed to take up this contentious issue. The Court's only detail following months of waiting was to say simply that "the petition for a writ of certiorari is granted."

The Supreme Court could have waited until it was further out of the limelight to consider the explosive issue in *Masterpiece Cakeshop* but chose not to. On another potentially polarizing topic, though, the justices' hands have been essentially forced. During the Court's 2017 term, the Court will decide if partisan considerations in drawing voting districts for state and federal elections can ever run afoul of the Constitution. That is an issue that has confounded the justices for more than thirty years. In previous cases, the justices have been bitterly split over whether such political considerations can go too far. Redistricting—the practice of drawing voting districts—is traditionally done by state legislatures. Given the partisan context in which the district lines are drawn, partisan tinkering with districts is nearly as old as the country itself, defenders of the practice say. But partisan gerrymandering has led to the extreme divisiveness that has come to epitomize our politics today, challengers of the practice say. Moreover, they argue, if taken to the extreme, disfavoring voters simply because of which political party they affiliate with can violate the First Amendment's protections of the right to free speech and to freely associate with chosen groups. By a slim majority, the Supreme Court has agreed with the latter argument—that partisan gerrymandering, although a longstanding and widespread practice—can go too far.

The problem for the Court has been finding how to measure when such considerations cross the line. Notably, in 2004, the Court split 4–1–4 over this question. Four conservative justices did not think that partisan considerations could ever run afoul of the Constitution and did not think there was a reliable, nonpartisan way to measure such considerations anyway. Four liberal justices thought not only that political considerations could go too far but also that they had found a way to measure such a circumstance. Those justices could not agree on what that measure was, though, putting forth three possible measurements, none of which garnered enough votes to become the law of the land. In the middle was Justice Kennedy. Kennedy still believed that political considerations in redistricting could be offensive to the Constitution, but he was not convinced that the measures put forth were dependable enough. For thirteen years, the issue has remained unresolved.

But now Wisconsin Democrats think they have found a way to sway Justice Kennedy, and they will make their argument next term in *Gill v. Whitford*. By using the so-called efficiency gap, courts can see when and how much party voters have been disadvantaged by the ruling political party. The efficiency gap—developed by liberal-leaning professors who are now involved in the challenge against Wisconsin Republicans—measures the number of "wasted votes" in any given election. Wasted votes include all votes cast in favor of the losing party and all votes cast in excess of the 50-percent-plus-one vote needed to win an election. To see why those votes are "wasted," it is important to understand how partisan gerrymandering takes place. The two most popular methods are "packing" and "cracking." Packing refers to the practice of cramming a large numbers of voters from one political party into a single district, so that all their voting power will be used to elect just one candidate from their preferred party. (If, by contrast, these voters were divided between two voting districts, the outcome might be the election of two representatives from their preferred party.) *Cracking* refers to just the opposite—dividing up voters from one political party into two or more districts so that they cannot reach a majority.

Packing and cracking was widespread in Wisconsin following the 2010 census, the challengers in *Gill v. Whitford* say. Following each decennial census, states undergo a process of drawing new voting districts to ensure that they account for major shifts in the population. The nationwide strategy among Republicans following the 2010 census was to draw voting lines that would maximize Republican control of both the state and federal governments. Wisconsin shows Republicans' tremendous success with that strategy. "In 2012, Republicans won a supermajority of sixty seats (out of ninety-nine) while losing the statewide vote," the challengers in *Gill* said in their Supreme Court filings. In 2014, "Republicans extended their advantage to sixty-three [seats] . . . even though the statewide vote remained nearly tied. Republicans thus wield legislative power unearned by their actual appeal to Wisconsin's voters."

Partisan gerrymandering, though, is not unique to Republicans, though they recently seem to have done a better job of exploiting it for their own advantage. Significantly, another partisan gerrymandering case that has already reached the justices—albeit on a procedural issue—was brought by Maryland Republicans who say they were unconstitutionally harmed simply because of the political party that they affiliate with. Notably, one of President Barack Obama's priorities after leaving office has been to make Democrats more competitive at partisan gerrymandering. Headed by former attorney general Eric Holder, the National Democratic Redistricting Committee has recently been founded to achieve on this goal.

The Supreme Court, though, could put the brakes on that effort by curbing partisan gerrymandering and drastically altering the way states approach redistricting. The Court, though, may not have wanted to. Most of the cases that come to the Supreme Court come through its so-called certiorari docket. In those cases, the justices have complete discretion to hear or turn away a case. The decision to do the latter sets no legal precedent and the justices have frequently admonished that such decisions in no way suggest agreement with the lower courts' decisions. That is not the way it used to be, however. Traditionally, the Court carried a much heavier caseload, as the Court was required to hear most cases that were appealed to it. Known as an automatic appeal, Congress significantly cut back on this practice during the 1900s, resulting in the current system we have today. But for issues considered imperative to the democratic functioning of our government, the automatic appeal still applies. Redistricting is one such issue. The chief justice has lamented that this essentially forces the justices to hear redistricting cases when they otherwise would turn them away. While the Court can act summarily in these cases, doing so sets precedent for lower courts in a way that turning away a certiorari case does not. Such was the case with *Gill v. Whitford*.

The case—along with the other hot-button issues that the Supreme Court has agreed to tackle in its 2017 term—threatens to once again cast the Court as a political institution. Of course, the appearance of being political arguably created the crisis in which the justices found themselves during the 2016 term—namely, a bitter political nomination process forcing a shorthanded Court to take on fewer and less controversial cases in order to avoid deadlocked outcomes. But fear of the next crisis does not seem to be inspiring any concern on the part of the justices. As William Baude put it in a June wrap-up for the Supreme Court's term in the *New York Times*, it looks as though the Court's 2016 docket may end up being remembered as a brief moment of calm before yet another storm.

Appendix

Biographies of Current Justices of the Supreme Court

All biographies are derived from the US Supreme Court website: https://www.supremecourt.gov/about/biographies.aspx

Chief Justice

John G. Roberts Jr., chief justice of the United States, was born in Buffalo, New York, on January 27, 1955. He married Jane Marie Sullivan in 1996, and they have two children—Josephine and Jack. He received an AB from Harvard College in 1976 and a JD from Harvard Law School in 1979. He served as a law clerk for Judge Henry J. Friendly of the US Court of Appeals for the Second Circuit from 1979 to 1980 and as a law clerk for then associate justice William H. Rehnquist of the Supreme Court of the United States during the 1980 term. He was special assistant to the attorney general, US Department of Justice from 1981 to 1982, associate counsel to President Ronald Reagan, White House Counsel's Office from 1982 to

1986, and principal deputy solicitor general, US Department of Justice from 1989 to 1993. From 1986 to 1989 and 1993 to 2003, he practiced law in Washington, DC. He was appointed to the US Court of Appeals for the District of Columbia Circuit in 2003. President George W. Bush nominated him as chief justice of the United States, and he took his seat on September 29, 2005.

Associate Justices

All justices are listed in descending order of seniority.

Anthony M. Kennedy was born in Sacramento, California, on July 23, 1936. He married Mary Davis and has three children. He received his BA from Stanford University and the London School of Economics and his LLB from Harvard Law School. He was in private practice in San Francisco, California, from 1961 to 1963, as well as in Sacramento, California, from 1963 to 1975. From 1965 to 1988, he was a professor of constitutional law at the McGeorge School of Law, University of the Pacific. He has served in numerous positions during his career, including as a member of the California Army National Guard in 1961, on the board of the Federal Judicial Center from 1987 to 1988, and on two committees of the Judicial Conference of the United States: the Advisory Panel on Financial Disclosure Reports and Judicial Activities (subsequently renamed the Advisory Committee on Codes of Conduct) from 1979 to 1987 and the Committee on Pacific Territories from 1979 to 1990, which he chaired from 1982 to 1990. He was appointed to the US Court of Appeals for the Ninth Circuit in 1975. President Reagan nominated him as an associate justice of the Supreme Court, and he took his seat on February 18, 1988.

Clarence Thomas was born in the Pinpoint community near Savannah, Georgia, on June 23, 1948. He attended Conception Seminary from 1967 to 1968 and received an AB, cum laude, from Holy Cross College in 1971 and a JD from Yale Law School in 1974. He was admitted to law practice in Missouri in 1974 and served as an assistant attorney general of Missouri, 1974–1977; as an attorney with the Monsanto Company, 1977–1979; and as a legislative assistant to Senator John Danforth, 1979–1981. From 1981 to 1982, he served as assistant secretary for civil rights in the US Department of Education, and he served as chairman of the US Equal Employment Opportunity Commission from 1982 to 1990. From 1990 to 1991, he served as a judge on the US Court of Appeals for the District of Columbia Circuit. President Bush nominated him as an associate justice of the Supreme Court, and he took his seat on October 23, 1991. He married Virginia Lamp on May 30, 1987, and has one child, Jamal Adeen, by a previous marriage.

Ruth Bader Ginsburg was born in Brooklyn, New York, on March 15, 1933. She married Martin D. Ginsburg in 1954 and has a daughter, Jane, and a son, James. She received her BA from Cornell University, attended Harvard Law School, and received her LLB from Columbia Law School. She served as a law clerk to the Honorable

Edmund L. Palmieri, judge of the US District Court for the Southern District of New York, from 1959 to 1961. From 1961 to 1963, she was a research associate and then associate director of the Columbia Law School Project on International Procedure. She was a professor of law at Rutgers University School of Law from 1963 to 1972 and Columbia Law School from 1972 to 1980 and served as a fellow at the Center for Advanced Study in the Behavioral Sciences in Stanford, California, from 1977 to 1978. In 1971, she was instrumental in launching the Women's Rights Project of the American Civil Liberties Union and served as the ACLU's general counsel from 1973 to 1980 and on the National Board of Directors from 1974 to 1980. She was appointed a judge of the US Court of Appeals for the District of Columbia Circuit in 1980. President Clinton nominated her as an associate justice of the Supreme Court, and she took her seat on August 10, 1993.

Stephen G. Breyer was born in San Francisco, California, on August 15, 1938. He married Joanna Hare in 1967 and has three children—Chloe, Nell, and Michael. He received an AB from Stanford University; a BA from Magdalen College, Oxford; and an LLB from Harvard Law School. He served as a law clerk to Justice Arthur Goldberg of the Supreme Court of the United States during the 1964 term; as a special assistant to the assistant US attorney general for antitrust, 1965–1967; as an assistant special prosecutor of the Watergate Special Prosecution Force, 1973; as special counsel of the US Senate Judiciary Committee, 1974–1975; and as chief counsel of the committee, 1979–1980. He was an assistant professor,

professor of law, and lecturer at Harvard Law School, 1967–1994; a professor at the Harvard University Kennedy School of Government, 1977–1980; and a visiting professor at the College of Law, Sydney, Australia, and at the University of Rome. From 1980 to 1990, he served as a judge of the US Court of Appeals for the First Circuit, and he continued as its chief judge, 1990–1994. He also served as a member of the Judicial Conference of the United States, 1990–1994, and on the US Sentencing Commission, 1985–1989. President Clinton nominated him as an associate justice of the Supreme Court, and he took his seat on August 3, 1994.

Samuel A. Alito Jr. was born in Trenton, New Jersey, on April 1, 1950. He married Martha-Ann Bomgardner in 1985 and has two children—Philip and Laura. He served as a law clerk for Leonard I. Garth of the US Court of Appeals for the Third Circuit from 1976 to 1977. He was assistant US attorney, District of New Jersey, 1977–1981; assistant to the solicitor general, US Department of Justice, 1981–1985; deputy assistant attorney general, US Department of Justice, 1985–1987; and US attorney, District of New Jersey, 1987–1990. He was appointed to the US Court of Appeals for the Third Circuit in 1990. President George W. Bush nominated him as an associate justice of the Supreme Court, and he took his seat on January 31, 2006.

Sonia Sotomayor was born in Bronx, New York, on June 25, 1954. She earned a BA in 1976 from Princeton University, graduating summa cum laude and receiving the university's highest academic honor. In 1979, she earned a JD from Yale Law School, where she served as an editor of the *Yale Law Journal*. She served as assistant district attorney in the New York County District Attorney's Office from 1979 to 1984. She then litigated international commercial matters in New York City at Pavia and Harcourt, where she served as an associate and then partner from 1984 to 1992. In 1991, President George H. W. Bush nominated her to the US District Court, Southern District of New York, and she served in that role from 1992 to 1998. She served as a judge on the US Court of Appeals for the Second Circuit from 1998 to 2009. President Barack Obama nominated her as an associate justice of the Supreme Court on May 26, 2009, and she assumed this role on August 8, 2009.

Elena Kagan was born in New York, New York, on April 28, 1960. She received an AB from Princeton in 1981, an MPhil from Oxford in 1983, and a JD from Harvard Law School in 1986. She clerked for Judge Abner Mikva of the US Court of Appeals for the DC Circuit from 1986 to 1987 and for Justice Thurgood Marshall of the US Supreme Court during the 1987 term. After briefly practicing law at a Washington, DC, law firm, she became a law professor, first at the University of Chicago Law School and later at Harvard Law School. She also served for four years in the Clinton administration as associate counsel to the president and then as deputy assistant to the president for domestic policy. Between 2003 and 2009, she served as the dean of Harvard Law School. In 2009, President Obama nominated her as the solicitor general of the United States. A year later, the president nominated her as an associate justice of the Supreme Court on May 10, 2010. She took her seat on August 7, 2010.

Neil M. Gorsuch was born in Denver, Colorado, on August 29, 1967. He and his wife, Louise, have two daughters. He received a BA from Columbia University, a JD from Harvard Law School, and a DPhil from Oxford University. He served as a law clerk to Judge David B. Sentelle of the US Court of Appeals for the District of Columbia Circuit and as a law clerk to Justice Byron White and Justice Anthony M. Kennedy of the Supreme Court of the United States. From 1995 to 2005, he was in private practice, and from 2005 to 2006, he was principal deputy associate attorney general at the US Department of Justice. He was appointed to the US Court of Appeals for the Tenth Circuit in 2006. He served on the Standing Committee on Rules for Practice and Procedure of the US Judicial Conference and as chairman of the Advisory Committee on Rules of Appellate Procedure. He taught at the University of Colorado Law School. President Donald J. Trump nominated him as an associate justice of the Supreme Court, and he took his seat on April 10, 2017.

Retired Justices

All justices are listed in order of retirement.

Sandra Day O'Connor, associate justice, was born in El Paso, Texas, on March 26, 1930. She married John Jay O'Connor III in 1952 and has three sons—Scott, Brian, and Jay. She received her BA and LLB from Stanford University. She served as deputy county attorney of San Mateo County, California, from 1952 to 1953 and as a civilian attorney for the Quartermaster Market Center, Frankfurt, Germany, from 1954 to 1957. From 1958 to 1960, she practiced law in Maryvale, Arizona, and served as assistant attorney general of Arizona from 1965 to 1969. She was appointed to the Arizona State Senate in 1969 and was subsequently reelected twice for two-year terms. In 1975, she was elected judge of the Maricopa County Superior Court and served until 1979, when she was appointed to the Arizona Court of Appeals. President Reagan nominated her as an associate justice of the Supreme Court, and she took her seat on September 25, 1981. Justice O'Connor retired from the Supreme Court on January 31, 2006.

David H. Souter, associate justice, was born in Melrose, Massachusetts, on September 17, 1939. He graduated from Harvard College, from which he received his AB. After two years as a Rhodes Scholar at Magdalen College, Oxford, he received an AB in jurisprudence from Oxford University and an MA in 1989. After receiving an LLB from Harvard Law School, he was an associate at Orr and Reno in Concord, New Hampshire, from 1966 to 1968, when he became an assistant attorney general of New Hampshire. In 1971, he became deputy attorney general and, in 1976, attorney general of New Hampshire. In 1978, he was named an associate justice of the Superior Court of New Hampshire and was appointed to the Supreme Court of New Hampshire as an associate justice in 1983. He became a judge of the US Court of Appeals for the First Circuit on

May 25, 1990. President Bush nominated him as an associate justice of the Supreme Court, and he took his seat on October 9, 1990. Justice Souter retired from the Supreme Court on June 29, 2009.

John Paul Stevens, associate justice, was born in Chicago, Illinois, on April 20, 1920. He married Maryan Mulholland (deceased) and has four children—John Joseph, Kathryn, Elizabeth Jane, and Susan Roberta. He received an AB from the University of Chicago and a JD from Northwestern University School of Law. He served in the US Navy from 1942 to 1945 and was a law clerk to Justice Wiley Rutledge of the Supreme Court of the United States during the 1947 term. He was admitted to law practice in Illinois in 1949. He was associate counsel to the Subcommittee on the Study of Monopoly Power of the Judiciary Committee of the US House of Representatives, 1951–1952, and a member of the attorney general's National Committee to Study Antitrust Law, 1953–1955. He was second vice president of the Chicago Bar Association in 1970. From 1970 to 1975, he served as a judge of the US Court of Appeals for the Seventh Circuit. President Ford nominated him as an associate justice of the Supreme Court, and he took his seat on December 19, 1975. Justice Stevens retired from the Supreme Court on June 29, 2010.

Acknowledgments

This book would not have been possible without the constant encouragement and helpful guidance of my editor, Damon Linker. His patience in shepherding me though the process and his endless support in solidifying my murkier ideas were invaluable. I am greatly appreciative. Thanks too to Garrett Epps, who recommended me for this project. The collegial atmosphere created by Garrett and others in the Supreme Court press corps is delightful.

I cannot say enough about my colleagues at *Bloomberg BNA*, who were supportive of this endeavor from the moment it was presented. First, thanks to my bosses, Jessie Kamens and Tom Taylor, who not only helped guide me in this project but continuously and ceaselessly support my everyday coverage of the Supreme Court. I could not ask for two better people to work for. Countless other individuals at *Bloomberg BNA* were also—perhaps unknowingly—imperative to completion of this project. Special thanks are due to Nick Datlowe and Jordan Rubin, who helped me work though particularly troublesome aspects of the Court's history and terms.

Acknowledgments

Of course, I could not have undertaken this project without the support of my family. From my stepfather's helpful edits to my dad's willingness to watch my energetic children while I toiled away, my family members chipped in in whatever ways they could. Thanks especially to my partner, James Robinson, who as I write is suffering through yet another trip to Chuck E. Cheese's so that I can focus on this project. Everything I have accomplished in my adult life is attributable to his everlasting support and encouragement.

Finally, I would be remiss if I did not thank the readers who follow my Supreme Court coverage at *Bloomberg BNA*. Reporting on the high court has been an unexpectedly rewarding endeavor, and it would not be possible without your readership. It is truly a pleasure to keep you up to date on the news of the highest court in the land.

9 780812 249972